Peanut Butter Sticks To The Roof Of Your Mouth

Joan Howard

Dear Amy & Zak -
Hope you enjoy the
reading and the cooking -
Just call me if you have any questions!
Joan Howard

BookPartners
Wilsonville, Oregon

Copyright 1995 by Joan Howard
Illustrations Becky Woodard
All rights reserved
Printed in U.S.A.
Library of Congress Catalog 94-78435
ISBN 1-885221-10-X

BookPartners, Inc.
P. O. Box 922
Wilsonville, Oregon 97070

Dedication

This book is dedicated to all the people who over the last 30 years have shared their knowledge and love of food with me in kitchens throughout the Northwest. Your gifts have certainly made my sauces saucier, my heart warmer and my life richer.

You know who you are, and I thank you all.

Life sticks to your heart,
  Food sticks to your ribs,
   And ...
Peanut butter — well —
  Peanut butter sticks
    To the roof of your mouth.

Table of Contents

Introduction 1
Real Life Real Cooking .5
Picnics for People of All Sizes 13
    Ollie's Black Olive Sandwiches 17
Of Seas and Seafood 21
Backroads Bounty 27
Canning and Other Gifts from the Kitchen 33
    Herbed Garlic Mayonnaise 37
    Designer Oil 38
    Fragrant Vinegar 39
Reunions 41
    Official Cockburn Spread 47
    Patty's Ham with Asparagus 48
A Mushrooming Good Time 49
    Best-Ever Fried Morels 52
    Gourmet Sauce 53
    Seafood Sauce 54
Wilderness Cooking 55
    Birdseed 60
    Mountain Mush 61
A Northwest Gathering of Nuts 63
    Microwave Nut Nibbles 66
    Filbert Tips 66
Herb-o-Mania! Parsley, Sage, Rosemary
    and Thyme 67
    Pesto 69
    Pasta PrimaVera 69

Garlic Points 70
Herb Tips 70
A Touch of Garlic — A Taste of Onion 71
Baked Garlic 73
Clay Pot Baked Garlic Chicken 74
Onion Lover's Pie .76
A Jug Of Wine 77
Fireside Warm Mulled Wine 80
A Patchwork Quilt Of This and That ...
      And Baking Bread 81
After-Thoughts 85
One-Dish Meals and Potluck Fare 81
Sheepherder Spuds 92
Buckaroo Beans 93
Ham Loaf 94
Cindy's Chicken Enchiladas 95
Chicken with Forty Cloves of Garlic 96
Frijoles Borrachos (Drunken Beans) 97
Chicken Piccata 98
Onion Soup 99
Pasta, Pasta 101
Japanese Salad 102
Sesame Rice Noodles 103
Pasta Port Umatilla 104
White Beans and Pasta 105
Shrimp and Veggie Linguini 106
Northwest Clam Sauce Linguini 107
Seafood 109
Tillamook Bay Cheese Bake 110
Sole Fillets with an Extra Touch 111
Halibut with Almond Butter 112
Pesto Rotini and Shrimp 113
Wild Rice and Shrimp 114
Yakima Crab Cakes 115
Crabmeat Casserole 116

Crabmeat Imperial 117
Ron's Crab Dip 118
Potato Chip Dip 119
Sand Dabs with Tomatoes and Shallots 120
Breakfast 121
Larry's Breakfast Drink 122
German Pancakes 123
Fancy Egg Scramble 124
Bread 125
Barbequed Bread 126
Poppy Seed Coffee Cake 127
Angel Biscuits 128
Porcupine Bread 129
Flatbread 130
Dilly Casserole Bread 131
Old-fashioned Lemon Bread 132
Mother Walpole's Whole Wheat Bread 133
Joan's Enriched Bread 134
Cinnamon Rolls 135
Six-Weeks Treasure Muffins 136
Rhubarb Crumb Coffee Cake 137
Jam Bundt Cake 138
Refrigerator Rolls 139
Rich White Coffee Can Batter Bread 140
Quick Butter Croissants 141
Incidentals 143
Merle's Mop Sauce 144
Olive Pepper Caviar 145
Best Ever Beer Batter 146
Crème Fraîche 147
Dill-Mustard Sauce for Ham 148
Sweetened Condensed Milk 149
Steak Marinade 150
Summer Ice Cubes 151
Cucumber Salsa 152

Tortilla Chips 153
Canning and Gift Giving 155
   Bertha's Rhubarb-Strawberry Gelatin Jam . .156
   Sauerkraut 157
   Pickled Pig's Feet 158
   Rhubarb-Strawberry Puree 159
   Pickled Ginger 160
   Seafood Seasoning Mix 161
Desserts 163
   Coconut Cream Pie 164
   Mother Howard's Inimitable Chocolate Pie .165
   Pineapple Cheesecake 166
   Toll House Pie 168
   Orange Chiffon Pie 169
   Strawberry Pie 170
   Deluxe Chocolate Marshmallow Bars 171
   Chocolate Syrup Brownies with
      Chocolate Buttercream Frosting 172
   Fudge-Butterscotch Suicide Cake 173
   Christian Church Apple Crisp 174
   Blackberry Cobbler 175
   Iola's Oatmeal Cookies 176
   Gilded Lily Apple Crisp 177
   Barb's Molasses Cookies 178
   Pumpkin Squares 179

Introduction

We may live without poetry, music and art;
We may live without conscience and live without heart;
We may live without friends, we may live without books,
But civilized man cannot live without cooks.

Edward R. Bulwer-L

While I was at work on this book, people sometimes asked my why I was writing another cookbook? It seemed the best thing for me to write though. I love to cook and I discovered long ago that when you love what you're doing, it shows. (In my case, it usually shows on my hips and thighs.)

I also know that even people who hate to cook love to read cookbooks. There is something both soothing and seductive about sitting down in your favorite chair with a good cookbook contemplating the mysteries of how one cup of flour, one cup of shortening and a little ice water can magically be transformed into an irresistible, flaky piecrust.

In this book you will find some favorite recipes which I have chosen from among the many I have tried over three decades of life in the Pacific Northwest. You will also find stories about my family and friends and the treasures — straight from their hearts — they have handed me.

Common sense, good manners — to say nothing about organized religion — are the ingredients that have given me direction for life. My love for food and home has made my life rich and full and helped me over the rough spots in the road.

I often meet people who, whether natives or imports, share my love for the Northwest, and together we marvel over the mystique of this natural paradise. Curled against the shores of the Pacific Ocean — "from the mountains to the prairie, to the ocean white with foam" the Northwest thrives on its own magic and its incredible natural beauty. I am grateful I call this corner of the world my home.

First, one set of my great-grandparents came to the Northwest by wagon train and later on, my grandparents traveled by "iron horse." At the time they crossed this vast continent to settle in Washington and Oregon, there were no food processors or bread machines, no microwaves or self-cleaning ovens, no radicchio or nouvelle cuisine. For the settlers, cooking three square meals a day came down to the availability of ingredients and the practicality of preparation. From the depth of a glowing, hot wood stove, delicious pies and wholesome, fragrant breads emerged to tempt the palate of hard working farmers, and a heavy black skillet fried up just about anything from meat to fowl to fish.

You won't find anything too fancy here in the way of recipes. I have stayed pretty much with the old-fashioned ways — simple food that is easy to prepare and good to eat.

I hope you will enjoy the reading, the cooking, the eating and especially the sharing. I believe that the best part of food is the joy it gives to one's company.

Real Life and Real Cooking

I have always loved to eat. However, as a youngster I liked to cook almost as much as my mother liked to clean up after me which, judging from my own experience, could not have amounted to a hill of beans. At about age ten, though, I began noticing that everybody who came to the house gravitated to the kitchen. That's where the best stories and jokes were told, where information and bits of gossip were exchanged and where all that delicious food was cooked and often sampled well before serving.

The kitchen I love best comes with a generous supply of talented tasters, surreptitious snitchers, extra-curricula basters and the ever curious pot-peekers. One such fellow ruined a perfectly fine pot of my navy bean soup, by adding one teaspoon of ground cloves — the recipe called for a mere pinch. But, for the most part, I love to have my share of viewers and doers in the kitchen, even if the helpers just keep "sampling" the food.

I silently chuckle at the folks who show up in my kitchen at meal time — which is about anytime around my house — swear they're not hungry, confess to having a less than bird-like appetite, are on a diet, or are on their way out to dinner, yet manage to put away two helpings of my blue plate special.

One of the first kitchens in my adult life was a large room with lots of light pouring through a glass brick wall, where as a freshman college student, I set up my typewriter on the same oak table at which my mother had studied her lessons by the light of a coal oil lamp several decades earlier. On that solid hunk of well-used oak, I would happily punch out my term papers, punctuating my "timeless" prose with breaks for stirring a kettle of soup simmering away in a heavy Dutch oven.

Just around dinner time, I mysteriously managed to attract a neighbor or unsuspecting passer-by to share our meal. There's really nothing better on a blustery evening than digging into a big bowl of hot and hearty soup with a chunk of warm, crusty bread along with good company and lively conversation.

A few years after I left the university, with the memory of cramming for exams until dawn still in my blood, I developed a passion for midnight cooking and spent many late hours — wide awake — perfecting a terrific recipe for lasagna, whipping up some dangerously appetizing dips, and rolling out the lightest of yeast doughs for the best-ever cinnamon rolls.

I was often in the company of a good friend with the same strange nocturnal habits. I guess you could call us the kitchen vampires: rising at midnight, along with the yeast dough, taking chunks out of fluffy, mouth-watering cinnamon rolls and slipping back into bed before the first peek of the rising sun could catch us. We left the fruit of our labors on the kitchen counter for husbands who worked swing shifts, and were always gratified to return home to delicious snacks. (Was it love at first bite?)

Modern technology is about the only thing that causes me trouble in my kitchen. My neighbor, Rita, once brought me her food processor, hoping I could make the darn gadget chop up her cabbage for cole slaw. Two hours later, after trying every possible combination, settings and translating directions from the Chinese — which included holding one foot on the floor and praying to our ancestral Kitchen God, we chopped the now tired cabbage by hand. We finished the job with the help of a glass of wine and congratulated ourselves for being technologically advanced enough to run our dishwashers.

When the television series *Knots Landing* shot a sequence at Oregon's famous Salishan Lodge several years ago, I finagled an invitation to cover the story for a local magazine. The set included a lavish presentation of fabulous foods created by Salishan's famous chefs. I watched with horror as the film crew covered the painstakingly decorated, sumptuous dinner buffet with a layer of formaldehyde — so that salmon, salads and breads would hold up under the hot lights. As I watched the scene being shot again and again, I mourned the destruction of all that beautiful food and knew I would never again yearn to eat straight off the pages of *Bon Appetit* or *Gourmet* magazine.

With a thick layer of cooking oil to catch the light, and a dusting of chemicals to prevent self destruction, fish, fowl and fettuccini alike glow and shine on the glossy pages of food magazines. From advertising pages to feature articles, tables in spacious dining rooms gleam with silver, exquisite China and enough crystal stemware to make me glad that I'm not doing the dishes. That's what I call "designer food," nice to look at but hard to pronounce, and even more important — impossible to digest.

I have learned to appreciate the fact that even my most sumptuous dinners do not look anything like the cover of *Wine and Food* magazine. Instead, we eat our meals on grandma's treasured old oak table, where decades ago she fed hungry bunches of harvesters. A handful of bright flowers from a summer garden sits in the middle of the table, and with pride and joy, I serve our meals on my grandmother's old-fashioned pottery which is hand painted with quaint farm scenes. Many miles and many years later, I can still conjure up the meals I ate as a child at grandma's table just by holding one of those plates in my hand. Everything looks and tastes real. And like my memory, the aroma of food lingers on long after the meal has been consumed. This is real life and real cooking.

The table and the dishes have gone with me all over the Northwest and not only are part of my kitchen, but part of my life. And, life takes place in the kitchen, especially were I come from.

Everyone who comes to the house ends up in the kitchen. A friend drops in, settles down at the old oak table to lament a lost love, stays for dinner and — depending on the size of the heartache — on through breakfast. A weekend visitor rises early and joins me for breakfast, sharing coffee and secrets as a Dutch Baby rises to golden perfection in the oven, while innocent sleepy-heads slumber on in the other end of the house.

Late-nighters come into the kitchen to dry the last of the dishes and indulge in a leftover piece of cheesecake while we reminisce about shared childhoods and dream of the future. Cousins come to visit and over steaming cups of hot tea or coffee — while making notable inroads in a freshly-baked dish of death-by-chocolate brownies, or just-out-of-the-oven scones heaped with huckleberry jam — we talk about the family and solve the problems of the world. We laugh at our foolishness, we bemoan our losses, cry over broken romances, swallow our disappointments and bare our souls. We talk a lot about watching our weight, help our-selves to another piece of juicy apple pie and leave the worry about our body circumferences to the next day.

I also like my kitchen when I'm alone. Sitting quietly at grandma's table, I hear the old mantle clock tick com-fortingly and remember the story of how Uncle Gilbert had shipped it, carefully packed in Spanish Moss, from Florida to the Northwest for my parents' wedding gift. Now it reminds me of my heritage and my quirky, wonderful family that is spread from Milton-Freewater to the mid-Willamette Valley, from Spokane to Sacramento. They are all with me as I remember hot dogs roasted in the fireplace, family farm breakfasts of bacon, biscuits and eggs, huge holiday meals and tiny snitches from the-night-before pie. I remember them all as special occasions because they were shared with the folks I love and those who love me.

In spring I watch from my kitchen window as Mother Nature turns the Northwest into a young girl, dressed in filmy tutus of blossoms that float lazily down from their perches to blanket the fragrant shoots of new grass. The world is a riot of color as azaleas, tulips, daffodils, paper-white narcissus and my favorite hyacinths and pansies wiggle out of the ground to bask in the bright spring sun. Birds extol the grandeur of nature and I agree that spring in the Northwest is the best season of all.

In summer I rise early on a warm, bright morning to watch the wheat as it waves in a slight breeze and catch the sweet smell of the green-amber swirls as they ripen in the hot eastern Oregon sun. I remember the days I spent hauling wheat to the elevator in town, waiting for the combine to come around the field again as I worked on my tan from a ringside seat on top of our truck. Yes, summer in the Northwest is the best time of all.

In the fall I keep an eye out for the leaves to turn color. The dusty brown hills around me are suddenly painted with bright orange and red as Mother Nature takes a last fling with her paintbrush. Fall is also the very best time to walk the Oregon coast. The weather behaves better in autumn than at any other time of the year. I stroll along the sandy beaches dressed in a T-shirt and rolled-up jeans, gathering sand dollars while Tucker, my golden retriever, enthusiastically chases a flock of sea gulls. The fresh offshore breeze is laced with salt and sea, the sun is warm on my face and I remember that fall in the Northwest is the season I like best.

No sooner have the colors faded when the frenzy of holiday preparations begins and before I put away the Thanksgiving decorations, it's time to start baking boiled spice cakes and to locate the thermos — the one we fill with spicy hot apple cider to take along when we go out to cut our Christmas tree.

January always brings its share of gloomy days and dripping rain, perfect weather for baking a batch of bread, simmering a pot of soup or tasty stew, and putting my feet under grandma's table to rub Tucker's back. He's curled up into a big ball of fur, snoring softly probably dreaming about the fresh, new smells to sniff when those first crocuses start to pop their heads up through the moist, rich soil.

Oh, yes, now I remember — all the seasons in the Northwest I love best.

Picnics for People of All Sizes

Oh, tough as a steak was Yukon Jake,
Hard-boiled as a picnic egg.
Edward. E. Aramore, Jr.

The first problem with going on a picnic in the Northwest presents itself right at the start, and is a hard one to solve. The silent wilderness is as tempting as the rose-filled city park. There are trails to hike, waterfalls to watch, miles of beaches to walk and those secret places from last year's outings beg for attention. Northwest weather being what it is, you might even find your car to be a great spot while you wait for a small squall or a big blow to pass.

Whatever, picnics are the best excuse for getting out and getting together.

People love to picnic — it's in their genes. It means getting away from home, eating food that tastes better out-doors, is much more appealing when roasted over an open fire and being able to conveniently leave the calorie counter at home. Kids love picnics. They get away from home and eat things that are, well, strictly picnic.

I once discovered my daughter, Sarah, and several of her friends, clumped around a tree stump in our back yard. On the left-over tree they had placed an unwashed bunch of broccoli, a quart-jar of ranch dressing and a pineapple hacked into indescribable hunks — all of which, they explained, was a "picnic." Like mother, like daughter — Sarah will transform any given moment into a gathering of friends centered around food, indoors or out.

I am sure my daughter's idea for a picnic did not reflect Omar Khayyam's concept of "A loaf of bread, a jug of wine and thou" — perhaps the most popular of all phrases extolling the virtues of the picnic. Despite my abiding enthusiasm for Khayyam, I know better than to expect a day-old French loaf and some leftover Zinfandel to adequately complement even my extensive virtues while gamboling through the meadow.

If anything, gamboling being what it is, a picnic will bring out the hearty appetite of even the most petite reveler, because it often takes some time to get to the meadow before the gamboling can begin. While I love a picnic as much as the next person, I am aware of the hazards beyond visiting ants and crash diving yellow jackets. I have a few suggestions for picnickers — or the casual traveller — with children.

First, nothing quells the maternal instinct like faces full of dark, sticky crumbs attached to a chubby human missile launching itself over the car seat towards your new sundress. Purchase a quantity of packaged wipe-ups equal to the ages of your children multiplied by the number of states in the Union. Wipies come in handy for a variety of uses, including wiping your brow.

A more economic approach as I remember from before the invasion of hi-tech toss-always — my mother had her own brand of wipies. For the first eight years of my life she simply carried in her purse a slightly soapy wash rag tucked into a plastic bag. It served its purpose well, stood up under the strain of repeated scrubbing and ended up in the laundry for recycling, rather than in the trash. There just isn't enough oomph in a wipie to mop up a small soft-drink flood.

Avoid messy foods for traveling in the car. Kids of all ages love jerky and, since it is already dried, will not smell up your car nearly as much as the tuna fish sandwich stuffed surreptitiously into the spare tire well by a finicky eater. Also beware of cheese spreads in squeeze containers. Unless the target is a soda cracker, refrain your children from using it in retaliation to an attack from a water pistol. Your car could end up smelling like the inside of the Tillamook cheese factory.

Bottled pop is great, as long as you stick to the clear liquids and forego strawberry and grape, which will find their way into your beige upholstery and leave memorable off-color imprints. Here's my answer to the pop war:

Save the bottles after the first round, fill them a third full of lemonade and freeze them for the next trip. Before leaving, pour whatever liquid you are pushing that week over the frozen stuff and you will have cold juice well into the fourth hour of the trip, (about the time junior is dying of thirst and refusing to drink water — especially warm water).

Actually, most small travellers will eventually eat whatever you lob into the back seat of the car, including the gum you are trying to detach from the lining of you purse.

I seem to have more trouble getting the tribe not to eat in the car — a fact to which my upholstery attests.

I maintain a "Yellow Alert" for picnicking opportunities by keeping a container ready for picnics at a moment's notice. This carry-all is not a wicker hamper lined with a red-checkered cotton cloth and matching napkins straight from the pages of a Better-Homes-and-Picnics catalog. I use a hard plastic file box. This somewhat unromantic container holds and protects all the accoutrements needed for a well-organized, enjoyable impromptu picnic.

In my box are all the non-perishable and mostly non-edible items I have come to rely on for picnics. You will find a list of my "necessaries" on page 18 which also go with me on camping trips. I keep my box well-stocked and ready to go, hoping for any excuse to gambol.

My favorite foods to take to picnics include fried chicken (leftovers are welcome), black olive sandwiches (a family favorite and a real picnic treat), chips, Chills and Fever (cucumbers and onions marinated in vinegar), fruit and cookies. I oven-fry my chicken after shaking it in a paper bag with a combination of whole wheat and white flour, garlic and onion powders and snipped, fresh herbs such as parsley, chives and tarragon. While the coated chicken pieces bake on a rack placed over a cookie sheet in a 400 degree oven, I have time to slice cucumbers and onions into a plastic bowl and cover with rice wine vinegar and ice cubes. They'll marinate nicely en route to the picnic, ready to complement the chicken and sandwiches.

Don't wait for someone to invite you to go picnicking, don't worry about the weather and to heck with the ironing — just go! I can't count the times I've sat in the car munching black olive sandwiches during the height of a storm watching the wind-whipped waves swell into 10-foot walls of dark green glass, crest to snowy-white foam caps against a dark, slate-gray sky, and crash on to the shore in spent fury.

I remember huckleberry-picking picnics, mushroom-hunting outings and Fourth of July fireworks festivities at the city park — all an excuse for being outdoors. Food always tastes better *al fresco* and it recharges your batteries to roam the woods, share a sandwich with a scurrying squirrel, and wrap your heart around the apricot-gold and turquoise of a sunset on the beach.

To your favorite picnic spot take along Ollie's Black Olive Sandwiches:

Ollie's Black Olive Sandwiches

1 can (approx, 4 oz) chopped black olives
4 slices bread
mayonnaise
lettuce leaves

Clean the lettuce and wrap in paper towels before leaving for the picnic. Just before eating, open the olive can and squeeze most of the juice out of the olives. Take along a small plastic bowl, or in a paper bowl from your picnic necessity box, mix the can of olives with a scant tablespoon of mayonnaise from the squirt bottle you have prepared. Spread this mixture on two slices of the bread, add the lettuce and spread mayonnaise on the other two slices of bread. Cut the sandwiches in half and eat carefully — the filling is as gooey as it is good.

Picnic/Camping Supplies

In my picnic supply box I keep a vegetable peeler, French and paring knives, can and bottle openers and a corkscrew, an assortment of Zip-Lock plastic bags, a sheet of foil, a couple of leftover plastic produce sacks, a small cutting board, plastic tablecloth, a package of sturdy plastic flatware, paper plates, cups and napkins, matches and two telescoping hot-dog roasting sticks. A large serving spoon and a pancake turner are a necessity for me, and I also pack a six-compartment spice bottle which comes in handy.

These items always stay in my box, ready to go at a moment's notice. Mustard, ketchup and even mayonnaise in squeeze bottles stay in the refrigerator to be packed into the cooler, along with a plastic drink jug full of ice which I store in my freezer until departure time. I prepare a small jug for a two-person picnic and a gallon milk jug for the larger picnic crowd.

Take along a book to read on the way (unless you're driving, of course). Maybe you'll choose *The Wind In The Willows* — one of Sarah's and my favorite books — where Mole is introduced to the great outdoors by Rat, who appears "staggering under a fat, wicker luncheon basket ..."

"What's inside it?' asked the Mole, wiggling with curiosity.

"There's cold chicken inside it," replied the Rat briefly; 'coldtonguecoldhamcoldbeefpickledgherkinssalad-frenchrollscressandwidgespottedmeatgingerbeerlemon-adesodawater ...'

"Oh stop, stop,' cried the Mole in ecstasy, 'This is too much!"

I can't think of a better way to enjoy the great outdoors. Unlike shy Mole, I agree with Mae West's rather general statement — not solely pertaining to picnics — "Too much of a good thing is wonderful!"

That's just like a Northwest picnic.

Of Seas and Seafood

The sea will ebb and flow, and heaven show his face...
Shakespeare

I was born and raised on "the dry side" of the state, in eastern Oregon where water is a precious commodity not given to displays of extravagance like the mighty Columbia or the ocean's tides rushing in against our rugged shoreline. Couse Creek, the small tributary of the Walla Walla where I grew up, is less than a trickle compared to some of the wide and swift-running rivers of Oregon and Washington. Where I come from there are seas of wheat and corn, and rivers of rows of beans wave in the sun, cattle graze on acres and acres of lush, green grass, and the air, and the dust and the pastures are dry.

But no matter where Northwesterners call home, we love it all — the ocean, the rivers, the lakes, the forests, the mountains, the deserts, and the farmlands. And, like most of us, my parents loved the seashore and introduced me to the ocean when I was about two years old. Their movie camera recorded my first encounter with the endless sea.

I can be seen gleefully running out toward the water with sea gulls dipping and soaring above, crash-diving into the surf to pick up a tasty morsel. Suddenly a wave rushes toward the beach, threatens to close in on me and sends me hot-footing back toward dry land, eyes and mouth wide open, bawling. An ignominious start for someone who has come to love the sea, not to mention seafood, with wild abandon.

Not being one to hold a grudge, I got over my first frightening encounter with the blue Pacific and developed a passion for walking the beach, anywhere from Anacortes to Brookings, in weather which can range from February's summer-like T-shirt days to the "most vile, thicke and stinking fogges" as described by Sir Francis Drake in 1597 when he sailed along the Pacific Coast, becoming one of the first if not the most appreciative of tourists.

Sir Francis notwithstanding, I love to watch the winter storms as they batter the rocks and hurl huge logs onto the beach with awe-inspiring force. It is a good reminder of my own relative smallness to see a tree stump as tall as a man, and as big around as a car lifted by the pounding surf and tossed about with the same ease I toss greens for a salad.

I even love to go deep-sea fishing, although the last few summers I have looked at the ocean and worried. The blue waters were dotted with boats of every size and description littering the horizon — looking suspiciously like the Los Angeles freeway system with fishing poles.

I grew up hearing tales of my own family's fishing exploits, some of which were accompanied by photos documenting the size of the catch. One snapshot shows Uncle Butch and my dad proudly holding up a five-foot string of trout caught on a trip to Canada. Another depicts Grandpa Sams with a 50-pound salmon he landed in Port Angeles in the days when you earned a pin for such a feat.

One of my favorite fish stories about Grandpa Sams is the "Sunday School Saga." Grandpa used to tell me that when he was little he and his brothers attended Sunday School faithfully. If the boys were very good at church on Sunday mornings in the late fall, they could skip the afternoon worship session in favor of riding their horses pell-mell up the creek, scaring the spawning salmon into jumping out on the bank. The boys would simply collect their scared-out-of-the-water booty in a gunny sack and head home for a salmon feast.

My mom must have gotten her love of fishing from her dad. I always loved the story about the time she hooked a nice fat trout, gave the line a good jerk, and flung her catch excitedly out of the water and directly behind her into the unexpectant face of the local game warden. By the time we get to the end of the story we are all hysterical with laughter so she never tells if she had her license. If, like grandpa, she had used a horse instead of a pole, she would have scared the poor fish ashore and dispensed with thrashing the local police.

I once went out over the bar with a group of seasoned sport fisher people. After the skipper motored past the bar he prodded me to "take the wheel" while he prepared the poles according to an elaborate scheme designed to catch lots of salmon or, at the very least, confuse all the other people fishing in the ocean.

This experience climaxed when the "Number One" fisherman, facing the back of the boat while untangling the lines, directed me to "Go left." I obliged in my best second mate fashion, being careful to turn slowly and not add more confusion to the already hopelessly tangled lines. The "Number One" fisherman uttered a selection of informative epithets as he worked on the fishing lines, looking up every so often to assess the horizon and shout over his shoulder "Go left." After several assessments and reminders to me to "Go left" and even to "Go left, *&%$ it!" the premier fisherman turned around, realized that since he was facing the back of the boat his left wasn't necessarily the *left* he wanted and furiously boomed out "No! No! The OTHER Left!"

Whatever happened to port and starboard?

Later on that same fishing trip, the seasoned fisher people experienced what is known as a "lull in the bite." This means the salmon, now stuffed with every kind of delicacy known to man, including several dozen soggy donuts haplessly dropped overboard by novice boaters, decided to take naps. The lull was filled with a discussion about the advantages and characteristics of various bait strategies, a discourse which elaborated the relative merits of blowing up worms with a syringe as opposed to heating Velveeta cheese in the microwave and rolling it in garlic powder.

As waves of seasickness washed over me, I could not decide whether to turn my fellow shipmates in to the Animal Humane Society or recommend them to Gourmets Anonymous.

Finally, however we arrived back at the dock and carted our catch of several beautiful Coho salmon back home. That's when my favorite part of the excursion began, the preparing and cooking of the salmon, the king of fish. Follow the simple and delicious recipes for cooking/baking/grilling salmon I've developed during my long love-affair with seafood. And there are other mouth watering sea critters for the dinner table: from tiny, plump and juicy Yaquina Bay oysters to freshly caught squid — known on the menu as calamari.

Here's how I fix calamari: After dipping the squid fillets in a beaten egg, coat it with a mixture of: one part finely ground almonds and three parts breadcrumbs. Firmly pat the coating mixture and saute quickly in a heavy skillet in hot butter. (No more than three minutes per side. What a treat!)

Rockfish and flounder, sea bass and perch all can be prepared like salmon — grilled, baked, fried or sauteed, with just a bit of lemon/dill butter. And when it comes to cracking freshly cooked Dungeness crab, dribbled with a bit of lemon-butter, accompanied by a crisp green salad and garlic points — well, that's living.

There is no end to the gifts from the sea — one of which is the boundless supply of food for the spirit to feast on. Whenever Tucker and I walk on the beach, where big Douglas firs crest the hillsides, where small firs, dwarfed and bent by westerly winds, crown bluffs and edge the wayside, and where dunes move inland ever so slowly and are reshaped by the furious breath of winter storms, I come alive.

Tucker races against the brisk offshore breeze, as though trying to fly with the sea gulls. He retrieves his stick from the edge of the surf and comes bounding back to me, panting and brown eyes begging for "one more throw, please."

People stroll at the edge of the water, eyes down, looking for those gifts the waves bring in from the depth of the ocean and spill onto the sand. Couples walk briskly hand in hand, heads held high facing into the wind, letting the strong breezes clear away the cobwebs of worry and fear.

Sometimes we poke around the shops and galleries in one of many small coastal communities looking at treasures made by men and sea — from kitsch to glorious art. Antiques and collectibles, heavenly trash and seawater taffy, glass balls from fishing fleets, shiny brass birds and yesterday's treasures are everywhere.

I stop at a small waterfront bakery where they serve hot cups of foamy cafe latte, strong, black espresso and steaming mugs of fragrant herbal tea along with delicious pastries no one can resist. Refreshed we return for one more look at the ocean.

The waves no longer scare me to death — I just don't turn my back on them.

Backroads Bounty

*"To own a bit of ground, to scratch it with a hoe,
to plant seeds, to watch their renewal of life —
this is the commonest delight of the race,
the most satisfactory thing a man can do."*
Charles Dudley Warner, 1871.

You can always tell the people who grow their own vegetables in the summer — they're the ones drinking zucchini Margaritas. If we could come up with the technology to make automobile fuel out of squash and zucchini, Kuwait and Saudi would never sell another barrel of oil to America. Sometimes I wonder if zucchini is not a weed we learned to eat because we couldn't kill it?

I know someone who at harvest time gets up in the middle of night, fills several big plastic buckets full of zucchini, all kinds of squash and lemon cucumbers, and under the cover of darkness drops them off at the front doors of strangers across town. (She had worn out her friends!)

She'd cut her headlights before she'd get out of the car, drop her load, get back into the car and turn on the lights when she was safely out of sight. She had tried to give her backyard bounty away to neighbors and friends, but, being true Northwesterners, they had their own burdens of vegetables to give away. You can make a lot of enemies by being too generous with your zucchini.

"Plant a toothpick, grow a tree," boasts a friend of mine, who came to the Northwest from a dry, hot Colorado town where little grew, and where early snows cheated her out of harvesting even one fully ripened apple from her one, lonely front yard tree. Northwesterners love gardening, although one friend of mine suggested that "gardening is for people with a cast-iron back with a hinge in it." She is the same person who has a hard time accepting the saying that "a weed is a flower in disguise," and when concerned with a friend's state of health, she wishes him the "bounce-back stamina of a dandelion."

But the real farmers, the ones who make their living and bet their future on a good harvest, look at it differently than the back yard gardener with too much zucchini on her hands. Farmers will tell you their job is exciting and romantic — a lot like gambling. They gamble on the wind, the rain and the snow, the heat and the sun, dry spells and hail, not enough of that and too much of this. They gamble on pesticides and weed-killers, and experiment with brand-new varieties of seeds which may or may not yield a bumper crop. In fact, farming is probably a bigger gamble than a trip to Las Vegas and that's a good thing because after they pay for the pesticides and the weed-killers and the big John Deer tractor and insurance and irrigation pipes, most farmers haven't a pocketbook left that would yield the funds for a trip to Vegas or anywhere else. It's a good thing that they can have all that fun while they're working.

Farming gets into your blood early. My Aunt Betty was about four years old when she started. Her parents, who were also my dad's parents, were living on the place our family refers to as "The Old Ranch." As a little girl, Aunt Betty saw her daddy and the other farmers planted tiny individual kernels of grain in the fall, and then watched as the little green shoots poked up through the ground the next spring and became beautiful stalks of wheat filled with lots of kernels of grain.

Auntie Betty had a pretty little ring she liked very much, and she thought it would be ever so nice if she had some more just like it. So she did what any farmer's daughter would do — she planted her ring.

She told me the story with a twinkle in her eyes, commenting that "it seemed logical at the time." The "seed" ring was never found to the young girl's and her mother's disappointment. However, Aunt Betty did not let that early experience diminish her enthusiasm for farming. With great fun she still plants the grain each fall and faithfully waits for the new little shoots to come up in the spring, which they almost always do.

I interviewed another enthusiastic farmer once, by the name of Warren, who did all his gardening organically and claimed to be able to kill potato bugs with a homemade concoction he creatively dubbed "Warren's Worm Slurry." He made the stuff secretly in his wife's blender when she wasn't looking. He then poured the mixture around the bases of the plants threatened by the nasty things. I don't know about potato bugs but that evil-smelling stuff would certainly deter me.

Warren also invented a novel method of discouraging birds from eating the cherries off his tree. He sent away to an organic gardening catalog for a drape that would prevent the birds from getting at the cherries. But by the time the cherries started to turn succulent red and the drape hadn't arrived, Warren decided to improvise. Lurking in his wife's canning pantry — again when she wasn't looking — (she really wasn't very observant) he ran across a bolt of cheese-cloth she had purchased for straining the summer's quantity of blackberry jam. Warren took the bolt out to the tree, tossed it high in the air a couple of times and decided, when it fell back and hit him in the head, that he would need some help. Any kid with a background in teepee-ing his girl friend's yard, could have acted as an on-hand consultant.

Warren festooned the cherry tree with the illegally acquired cheesecloth as he dangled from a high branch in the neighboring black walnut tree, held aloft by a rope run through a block and tackle and attached at the other end to the milk cow, Bessie. The complacent bovine compliantly but inadvertently moved Warren around the tree so he could cover all the cherries as she grazed contentedly in the south pasture. Ingenious!

I have tried in vain to erase the picture of Warren swaying dangerously high atop the cherry tree from my mind. It's stories like this that make gambling appear to be a perfectly plausible and safe occupation. But try and tell that to a farmer!

The love for growing things coupled with the Northwest's favorable growing conditions have produced an army of entrepreneurial backyard farmers who sell their excess produce at roadside stands, from the rear of pickup trucks and station wagons with the tail gate down, from under beach umbrellas planted unceremoniously in vacant lots. Each community sprouts its own colorful version of a farmers market, including formal Saturday Markets. I go to all of them!

I have become a backroads bounty-hunting junkie. After garage and yard sale and apres-Christmas bargain forages only a farmers market holds me in its spell. I can find my way to roadside stands and small markets with the accuracy of a bloodhound tracking a lost soul. Driving down a country road, my car automatically turns swiftly into that narrow private lane — directed by the slightly wavering arrow on a hand-painted sign which points to a farmhouse hidden behind a cluster of trees. Crooked red letters announce: PEACHES - CORN - APPLES - BERRIES--U-Pick or We-Pick — and I follow.

I frequent truck farms, Saturday Markets, stop at roadside stands, peek under umbrellas and grope around the tailgates of station wagons and pick-ups with faithful regularity, and in the course of my meanderings carelessly acquire large quantities of fresh fruit, vegetables, berries and bunches of fresh flowers. I arrive home loaded with three-times re-used paper bags, and cut-off cartons all filled to overflowing with the astounding varieties of things that grow in the dirt, in pots, on bushes and trees in our Northwest — the Garden of Eden.

I love the people I meet at my backyard bounty hunting. With a baby asleep next to her, a young woman is surrounded by baskets of dried status, strawflowers, bouquets of preserved rosebuds, and decorative weeds next to a tray of golden honey-straight from the bee hive, and a small mountain of saran-wrapped packages of fluffy home-made biscuits and zucchini-nut breads.

I love to chat with backyard farmers, and the growers and caretakers of the land. Young fresh faces with golden summer tans, and older faces with deep wrinkles crisscrossing weathered skin with apple-red cheeks are bent over baskets and boxes carefully rearranging their wares to show off the best, the ripest, the biggest and the most tempting fruits and vegetables. Hand-painted signs announce the price of things — freshly picked and fragrant, they always cost less than what you pay at the supermarket.

These people are the Northwest. Earthbound and wise to the land, they represent the honorable traditions of farming, of growing things and they understand the relationship of men and nature. Hard-working, proud of their efforts, honest and simple in their ways, they are only too glad to offer hints and tips for growing a garden as well as preparing and storing produce.

Gracious and eager to please, just as I'm ready to say goodbye, they reach for a big piece of fruit or a cookie, and with a generous gesture offer it as a parting gift. Their genuine warmth and easy laughter follow me home.

Canning and Other Gifts from the Kitchen

Or: ask me if I can can and I'll answer of course, I can can!

There are some things in life that are monumentally more satisfying than others — and canning is one of them. What is more gratifying — or beautiful — than a pantry filled with rows and rows of jars glowing in jewel-like colors, ready to brighten the table on a gloomy winter day and satisfy the heart and taste buds with the memories of warm and fragrant summers?

I love to go to friends' homes and watch them canning carefully selected batches of ripe, red tomatoes, golden, juicy peaches, fat, dark bing cherries and spicy pickles — and, not to forget the ever-present jars of zucchini relish.

Personally, I tend to can more unusual things. I once made 14 pints of "Red Beauty Preserves" which the recipe guaranteed would make any brunch a memorable occasion. But something went wrong, something was amiss with either the recipe or the cook. I ended up with an army of bloated red blobs floating lazily in 14 jars of gloppy red syrup. Not too good to eat; however, it was great for attracting yellow-jackets. Placed strategically around the patio, we enjoyed a bee-free summer, as the buzzing insects happily settled for the blood-red gunk instead of feeding off our dinner plates.

Not all of my canning and freezing exploits have been quite so disastrous. The year mom and dad brought a whole station wagon load of heads of cabbage from Pat and Win's garden in Joseph, I helped make an unbelievable number of quarts of the best sauerkraut I ever ate. Shredding a load of cabbage can make even the wiggliest ten-year old pay attention to business. Another time, I spent a Sunday morning one August cutting a pick-up truck load of corn off the cob and sealing it into quart-size plastic bags. That year we had summer all winter long every time we opened a bag of sweet yellow corn.

Another one of my favorite foods for preserving is tuna. It's a messy job but well worth the effort, especially if you own two canning pressure cookers — one can be cooling while the second one cooks. Adding a little vinegar to the cooking water keeps the house from smelling like the local fish processing plant.

No matter how simple the task — jams, jellies, fruits or pickles — home-canned goodies make wonderful gifts. A swatch of bright fabric cut with the pinking shears, a hand-lettered "Given with Love, from" label, a perky ribbon or silken cord dress up the jar and make welcome presents.

Among the home-made gifts I've received over the years is one special paper-mache article which doesn't look like much but is truly dear to me.

In the early 1920's, after my grandmother had been

teaching for long enough to be good at it, the State Teacher's Accreditation Board announced bluntly that all school teachers would have to meet certain standardization requirements and would have to spend a year at Normal School sprucing up their skills.

Grandmother lived on a farm, had a husband, a nine-year-old daughter who would later become my mother, and taught school. She had been using her quick mind, logic and on-the-job training skills with good results. Normal School was clear across the state and it took about two days to get there by car.

It was not yet fashionable for husbands to uproot their lives and livelihoods to follow the little woman cross country as she pursued her career. Moving a farm complete with house, barn, cows, pigs and vegetable garden would have been a might impractical. Grandmother was an intrepid soul and she and my mother traipsed across the state alone to live away from home for a year of book-learning and missing grandpa and Eastern Oregon a whole lot.

Grandmother, who could sing, play the piano and tell stories to rival Longfellow, did not "do" art. An art project was as simple a task for her class as cutting pictures out of the Monkey Ward catalog or using autumn leaves in a variety of artsy ways. However, to be accredited, grandmother had to complete an art project.

In resignation, she made an ephemera, or Effie — a brown and white cow — udders and horns painstakingly accurate. Ephemera is the antique dealer's term for stuff like old syrup tins, calendars with pictures of model T-Fords and faded Shredded Wheat cardboard boxes bearing the inscription "The Cleanest, Finest, Most Hygienic Food Factory In The World — Copyright 1911.

Ephemera also translates into an object that has a short life span. Mostly, the items were made from paper, tin or cartons and were meant to be tossed when their contents were used up. The paper-mache cow was, of course, paper and so it fit into the category.

Effie is now in my possession and brings me comfort and courage although its beauty remains obscure to others. When I'm depressed I take a look at Effie and remember what Grandma went through, and that helps to make me deal with whatever ails my heart — short-lived as the pain may be.

Effie, the cow was the start of a growing collection. After I acquired the paper mache idol — over Grandma's protests — I got interested in other pieces of ephemera, such as the Wesson Oil Mayonnaise Maker I found in an antique shop a few years ago. It is a glass jar with a slotted metal plunger inside and a handle which goes through a hole in the lid. Into the jar you pop the eggs, seasonings and oil, up and down goes the plunger and out comes mayonnaise. I used it once to make sure it worked, then retired it lovingly on the shelf near Effie.

I don't have grandma's formula for paper mache, but here are some recipes for welcome gifts from your kitchen that will be greeted with oohs and ahhs of delight and gratitude.

Herbed Garlic Mayonnaise

I've even made a deliciously different mayonnaise by adding some garlic and an herb or two. You may follow standard recipes for making from scratch-mayo, or, you can use prepared mayonnaise:

1 cup mayonnaise (shortcut)
1/2 teaspoon finely chopped garlic
1/4 teaspoon chopped basil
1/2 teaspoon tarragon

Mix well, serve with fish or use as sandwich spread. For one more flavor change to serve with baked or sauteed fish fillets, add 1 tablespoon capers and 1 tablespoon chopped fresh parsley — it's deliciously sophisticated.

~ ~ ~

Designer Oil

Prepare a slender, decorative glass bottle that holds approximately 1 cup of liquid by rinsing it with boiling water and letting it dry. Prepare and place in bottle:

1 carrot stick
1 celery stick
2 peeled cloves garlic
2 pearl onions
1 slim 2 inch, piece of lemon peel
1 leaf fresh basil

Fill to top with a good quality, extra virgin olive oil. Cork and add decorative cord.

Fragrant Vinegar

Prepare a decorative quart glass bottle as for Veggie Oil.

Use one or two wooden skewers. On each skewer assemble:

1 clove garlic
1 green pitted olive
2 pearl onions
1 small chunk carrot
I small chunk fennel root
1 sprig fresh tarragon

Place skewers into bottle, fill with white vinegar, cork, decorate with silk or metal cord.

~ ~ ~

You don't have to knit your own sheep from strands of clouds and bits of moss — one molecule at a time — or gold leaf a batch of brownies and store them in a hand-painted box you made from an old lampshade, to make gifts from your kitchen that please. Whether it is a small basket filled with dried summer flowers, a jar of zucchini relish, (here we go again) or a crock of tart and sweet mustard made by you — they are the best kind of gifts.

Reunions

Family jokes,
Though rightly cursed by strangers,
Are the bonds that keep most families alive.
Stella Benson

Each year I look forward to our family reunion. Some of my family members are from around the old homestead, others like me, moved away, but we happily pick up kid and kaboodle along with the family dog, pack plastic containers full of pickles, olives, cole slaw, chicken, casseroles, pies, sticky buns and salads, deviled eggs, rolls and baked beans and head out.

In spite of the ever-present bags of chips and somebody's idea of clam dip there's almost always some little gem of a dish to be discovered. It may be an unusual salad, an exotic main dish or fabulous dessert, which demands that I force myself to take a second helping. Then there are the recognizable and memorable dishes that are standard contributions by the same aunts and cousins — because they are so good! And more than that, in addition to all those wonderful recipes (my family tries to out-do each other in the kitchen), I am also likely to collect some priceless family gossip.

Time to see everyone, time to catch up with the folks. Few of us are good letter writers anymore, and word of mouth by telephone is limited to important news — like deaths and births. I get to see all my cousins and their off-spring, see who lost weight or gained some since last year, and what haircuts and colors are in vogue.

I look around me and see a few more lines in some of the familiar faces — including mine; a pair of eyes reflect pain that sparkled with joy just last year. I watch some of the older relatives walk a bit more carefully, not quite as erect. Hands that once held firm the reins of homes and farms show signs of aging, and there is a subtle letting-go in the way they hold their head. But their hearts are young and defy the encroaching years. And they come to see every-body, and they visit and chat as they wistfully — and at times boisterously — reminisce. We all love it.

And then there is the next generation, full of mischief, adventure, shrieks and happy laughter — running, tum-bling, tearing around, racing from one activity to the next, with enough energy to recharge us all.

"Boy, wouldn't I want to have some of that energy," someone comments wistfully, eyelids dropping slowly over tired eyes for a quick nap. I look at several of my aunts and remember my favorite story about them, which someone is sure to tell again.

Astonishing as it may seem, my aunts, known to me as proper matrons always attired in suits, hose, pearls and patent leather pocketbooks, were once little girls. When they were kids, the neighboring town of Athena hosted an annual Scottish gathering, referred to as Caledonian Days. Bagpipes skirled to announce the festivities, and dancing contests were held throughout the day as the picnic progressed from noon to night. It was a gay and colorful event. My aunts, curious and clever girls, would lie on their backs in the grass near the serving tables and hope for a kilted Scot to happen by to assist them in their research as to what those bagpipers wore under their scratchy, short wool kilts. They claim they never found out and neither have I.

My family has had a few Scottish gatherings since then, but minus the bagpipers. Just the same, we manage to provide a good bit of entertainment if only by exchange of stories, pictures, jokes and limericks.

Once, en route to one of the family gatherings in the car, someone wondered aloud if Barbara was prepared for the pack of relatives about to descend on her.

"Who's Barbara?" inquired 10-year old Elizabeth.

"She is our cousin who is hosting the party," her mother explained.

"Oh," Elizabeth replied — with her newly acquired knowledge from her biology class — "if she is the host, that must make us the parasites."

The girl's comments warranted a few appreciative chuckles and was added forever to the repertoire of family bon mots.

Family reunions are fun and are the one event where people remember the past and the days when they were young together. And maybe they meet to bear witness to the fact that they share the same gene pool and pretend they have certainly more in common than dead relatives. Funny thing is, the dead relatives are likely to show up — in the faces and bodies of their living descendants.

Uncles and aunts watch the antics of the youngest generation and each one searches with Sherlock Holmes-like diligence to find family likeness in the fresh new faces.

"Don't you think," they muse, "young so-and-so takes after our Jo — God rest his soul?" And, so-and-so favors her mother's first cousin — and someone else is cut from the same cloth as one of the dear departed. Another boy is pronounced the spit'n image of someone long gone.

At each reunion cousin Mac looks more and more like our Grandpa Mac — except for the ponytail and motorcycle leathers. And Jon's beautiful girls all have dark, snapping Cockburn eyes, giving us an animated glimpse of what our aunts really looked like as young girls, though we've only seen their pictures. Making comparisons and establishing resemblances is one way of immortalizing one's honorable ancestors, and just may assure us of our own way of living on.

And so it goes. I have discovered that if the members of my family live long enough, in the course of their lives, they will have "taken after" every one of their ancestors at one time or another.

Some things remain untouched by time: young boys still pull the girls' hair and chase them with frogs or snakes in hand; girls grab the snakes and chase the boys back. Little ones glide through the air on a rope-and-tire swing tied securely to a fat branch of a big cottonwood tree, shrieking with frightened delight. Young mothers compare babies and baby-raising advice and consolations... "Mine had colic all the time. Tried everything from peppermint to gin — you just have to let them outgrow it."

Good advice. It worked for Sarah and me.

Men still talk about crops and the weather, equipment and water problems, livestock and the price of wheat. They discuss going to church on Sunday, exchange tidbits about the new minister and his wife, the county fair and blue ribbons, last year's round-up, who passed on and how nice the funeral was. How about that wedding of the neighbor's daughter? — nice, but a bit hurried, don't you think? Those matters are still topics for conversation. Some things never change.

Photos come out of the woodwork and are passed around between sips of iced tea and pop, between bites of crisp, moist, fried chicken and tender golden corn. My favorite picture is the one of the old-world-Scottish patriarch Mac, known to us all as a stern, take-charge sort of a fellow, captured on film as he meekly sweeps the walkway in front of the newly-built family home. His wife Minnie watches imperiously from a few feet away, hands on hips, her stance clearly stating "You missed a spot."

In another photo from the late 1800s Andrew and Rebecca Cockburn sit amidst their children, my grandpa Mac among them, in the parlor of the family home. On the walls behind them are several paper calendars reminiscent of the time. If you look closely, you will see a painting of a seaside scene, hung by a string which has been hooked over a pen knife stuck into the door frame. As it happens, Barbara's sister-in-law gave her a copy of the same print. She had found it at a garage sale and recognized it from the family portrait. The seaside scene — this time a replica of the original — is now ceremoniously hung by the original penknife — on a door or window frame somewhere at all the tribal gatherings.

At one annual party, our reunion hostess, Lynn, was

putting finishing touches on a woven wire cage in the side yard just as I arrived. I wondered if she intended to confine out-of-control family members in the fragile structure of a wire cage? It turned out she and her husband Dewey were raising quail that year. I remembered stories of how the sight and sounds of those plump, swift birds were plentiful in the Milton countryside at the time our great-grandparents were growing up almost a century ago. No longer plentiful, thoughtful Lynn wanted to add to the population of the picturesque quail. They belonged to the landscape.

Sarah, an only child, always has a marvelous time with her cousins. They seem to enjoy each other's company once again as much — or maybe more than — the grownups. At one reunion I came upon her and another almost-teenager with their heads together sharing an obvious secret. It made me feel like I did when I was the littlest cousin and the big kids clammed up when I appeared, or they sent me to "get a drink of water" at the house while they told risque stories, or traded cigarettes or whatever.

I asked Sarah, what she and her cousin had been discussing. World Peace? Basketball? Rap music? No, she confided. They had a long talk after a careful observation of the folks around the tables and decided that there are a lot of fat genes in our family.

She's right! A lot of us Cockburns share the family trait of an ample, well-defined, hard-to-miss posterior. We jokingly call it "The Cockburn Spread." As we all eat and drink together during these reunions, it isn't hard to see why this is such a common, if un-enviable, similarity. Of course, the great recipes we all bring to the table — not just at family reunions — are part of the reason.

If you're having a potluck or a family reunion, or even

if you're not, here are a few of my favorites to help you put on a big spread!

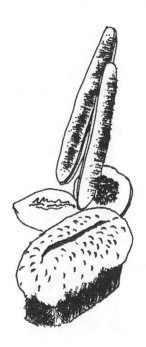

The Official Cockburn Spread

1 cup real bacon bits
2 cups sour cream
2 cups shredded cheddar cheese
1/2 cup chives, chopped fine
2 cups chopped smokehouse almonds
Blend ingredients, adding more sour cream if mixture is too stiff. Make a day ahead to allow flavors to mellow. Serve with chips, petite bread slices and raw veggies.

Patty's Ham with Asparagus

3 pounds cleaned asparagus
5 tablespoons butter
5 tablespoons flour
2-1/4 cups milk
Dash each salt, pepper and nutmeg
12 thin slices ham
6 hard-cooked eggs, sliced
1 cup grated cheddar cheese
1/2 cup grated swiss or monterey jack
Paprika

Steam asparagus until barely tender. Drain juice and add to measured milk. Melt butter in pan, add flour and stir until thickened. Add nutmeg, salt and pepper. In a 9" x 13" pan, layer half the asparagus, ham, eggs and 1/3 of the sauce. Repeat layers, ending with remaining sauce. Spread cheese over all, sprinkle with paprika and dot with additional butter if you like. Bake at 350 for 30 minutes. Let stand 10 minutes before serving.

A Mushrooming Good Time

He that high growth on cedars he bestow,
Gave also lowly mushrooms leave to grow.
Robert Souhwell, 1562-1595

In Provence and other parts of Europe the black truffle is emperor while the white truffle is king. The price for these pungent, musky fungi have reached astronomical heights and unless you have an unlisted Swiss bank account, you can come with me picking chanterelles and morels where the big firs block out the sky and the forest floor is alive with small critters, magic moss and — mushrooms. No pigs, no dogs, just you and I looking for Northwest "truffles."

Each year in the spring, I don my oldest jeans, grubbiest boots and most decrepit looking shirt and plow off into the hinterlands in search of — "seashells," because using the word "morels" is like using the Lord's name in vain.

I might run across a similarly-dressed couple carrying

brown paper sacks, walking around looking as though they lost their contact lenses — backs bent, eyes low to the ground and worried frowns on their faces.

I smile, say "Hi" and inquire after their health.

"Oh, fine, fine" the fellow responds defensively, gripping his wife's arm. "Me 'n the missus is just out for a little stroll, pickin' up pine cones for those wreaths she makes at Christmas time."

Right. I know. I'm looking for sand dollars, myself!

If you have never had the pleasure of eating morel mushrooms dipped in egg and cracker crumbs and fried to a golden brown, you'd know why perfectly honest, upright Northwesterners pull their hat brims low and lie like crazy about what's in the paper sack behind their back.

Why, seashells and sand dollars, of course.

In my family, you need security clearance to go mushroom hunting with the clan. Diligence and good eyesight are mandatory. And we usually blindfold newcomers the first time or two to make sure they won't discover the road to our favorite mushrooming patch. Woebetide the innocent who's grilled by a seasoned mushroom hunter about another fella's patch and carelessly discloses the sacred location. A slip of the tongue could blackball you for life.

But things are always changing. Recently the government got into the act and the forest service decided to regulate God's gift to mushroom lovers and requires the purchase of a mushroom gathering permit. Apparently morels have grown in popularity, fetch a pretty penny on the market and represent a multi-million dollar industry. There's that Northwest abundance again!

Every spring, as the mushroom season approaches — amidst mumbling and grumbling all sort of terms of non-endearments — I buy my mushroom gathering permit and head for the woods. Spring rains have washed the air clean and the fresh green of another spring is budding and bursting forth with new life. The earth smells heavy and rich, pungent and musty — just the place for morels to thrive. Ferns sprout new shoots and thrive in the dim light on the shadowy, moist forest floor. A few stems of snow-white trilliums nestle on a dew-covered mossy knoll. If I'm lucky, I'll see a few delicate, perfectly shaped lady slippers looking as if awaiting Cinderella's tiny feet. Sometimes I even come across a shooting star which my family calls "bird bills."

As I head for my secret place in the magic, fairy tale forest, I cautiously zigzag through the tall firs, flinging furtive glances over my shoulder to see if I've been followed. But all I see is an occasional squirrel scurrying up a tree and the bobbing tail of a lonely doe scampering out of sight.

Fat raindrops skid off a branch and land with a melodious wet plop on the ground in perfect harmony with the shrill squawking of blue jays and the melodious chirping of other feathered friends.

It's a perfect day for morel gathering while my heart and soul feed on the quiet beauty of the forest where life repeats and renews itself with an ever-present knowing. And I know, there's always another spring with its generous gifts heading my way.

There are very few main dishes that come to my table whose flavor can not be enriched by adding mushrooms to the cooking process. Here are a few of my favorite mushroom recipes. Your guests never have to know if the mushrooms were store-bought or home grown.

Best-Ever Fried Morels

1 pound fresh morels
1 box cracker crumbs
4 to 6 eggs, beaten together in a shallow pan
Vegetable oil

Soak morels briefly in lightly salted water. Drain well, shaking to remove most of the moisture. Roll in egg, then in cracker crumbs. Fry briefly — just until golden brown — on each side. Salt to taste before serving.

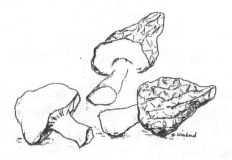

The European way to prepare morels is simply to saute the mushrooms in butter or margarine for about eight minutes, remove from skillet and sprinkle generously with freshly chopped parsley before serving. It's a side dish to honor both the elegant mushrooms, the main course and your dinner partners.

And for those who want to appear a mini-gourmet by serving a truly memorable sauce of big-time chef origin — try this — you'll love it and so will your guests.

Gourmet Sauce

To turn a steak dinner or a company roast into a feast:
In a heavy skillet

Saute 12 to 16 ounces of mushrooms, sliced
medium thick in 3 tablespoons butter for 5 minutes
Add a fourth of a cup of teriyaki sauce,
Cook to reduce liquid for 5 minutes medium high
Stir often.
Add 2 tablespoons of brandy, blend and serve over
meat
Six servings.

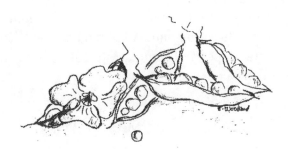

Seafood Sauce

To serve with grilled or baked salmon or other fish make the following sauce:

2 tablespoons butter or margarine
3 shallots, chopped fine
1 clove garlic, minced
1 small tomato, seeded and diced fine
8 ounces mushrooms, finely sliced
1 teaspoon ground ginger
2 tablespoons capers
3 tablespoons apple brandy
1/2 cup chicken broth
1 tablespoon lemon juice
1 tablespoon fresh Italian parsley, chopped

Saute shallots, garlic, tomato and mushrooms for about eight minutes.

Add chicken broth, simmer for about 10 minutes, or, until liquid is reduced by half. Add brandy. To thicken, stir in quickly 1 tablespoon of flour, avoid making lumps! Serve over fish.

Life is too short to stuff mushrooms.

Shirley Conran

Wilderness Cooking

"The man in the wilderness asked of me
How many strawberries grew in the sea.
I answered him as I thought good,
"As many as red herrings grow in the wood."
Nursery Rhyme

When Narcissa Whitman crossed the American Plains in 1836 she was the new bride of Marcus, a doctor and would-be missionary. But it was Narcissa and Eliza Spalding who were lauded "back east" when news of their successful journey finally reached civilization. Narcissa and Eliza were the first white women to cross the plains to the western United States.

Henry Spalding, Narcissa's spurned suitor and then husband to Eliza, recounts in his journal that on the Fourth of July these two intrepid females reached the Rockies and "alighting from their horses and kneeling on the other half of the continent, with the Bible in one hand and the American flag in the other, took possession of it as the home of American mothers ..."

Eliza, sickly through most of the journey and much less given to grand sentiment and prevarication than Henry, noted in her journal only that the group filed over the Divide and camped on a tributary of the Green River, to be surprised by a welcoming party of Indian braves later that evening.

Narcissa for her part treated the whole adventure as just that — marvelling in her letters and diary at being able to carry a knife in a scabbard on her belt, and retelling the story of entertaining some Englishmen in the caravan with tea cooked over a flame of dry buffalo dung which she compared favorably to the Pennsylvania coal she was familiar with. She also wrote of learning to bake bread in the open, making forks from sticks and delighting in buffalo meat..."I never saw anything like it to satisfy hunger ... I have eat three meals of it and it relishes well."

Mr. Spalding's grandiose and untrue statements notwithstanding, crossing the plains in the early 1830's was an ordeal. My own great-great grandmother, Martha Ann Graham Hastings, crossed the plains in 1862 with seven children, one of whom the lore goes, was in diapers. Not Pampers, but cloth flour sacks or calico. I am sure her mother tried hard to toilet train her during the journey whether it was good for her psyche or not.

When I was about twelve years old, my father arranged a four-day horse-back trip into the Eagle Gap Wilderness — which by the way, is often compared to the magnificence of the Swiss Alps — so that I might experience first-hand what he had grown to love as a young man. I knew I was right at home when I watched the newly-packed mule give in to a fit of bucking, tossing eggs, one, two and three at a time up, up in the air to come down with a splat. Here was a companion as clumsy with the cooking equipment as I was. The loss of the eggs meant no pancakes. It was no loss to me but a blessing, because I prefer biscuits.

Aside from the mule juggling the eggs, I don't remember a thing about food on that trip. I was too awe-struck with the beauty of the wilderness to think about food. Although I'm sure we ate well. I do remember Dad and the packer using a heavy cast iron skillet for cooking over the open fire — probably no different than the pioneers prepared their meals a century and more before.

On that first wilderness trip I saw my father dive head-first into a mountain stream and emerge seconds later with a hoot and a holler that was sure to start an avalanche. Diving into a glacier-fed lake is guaranteed to wake every-one within hearing distance, including the dead. We all bathed quickly — accompanied by shouts and shrieks — in the frigid waters and eagerly scampered back out onto the nearest granite boulder to dry in the reviving warmth of the sun.

In a landscape of incredible beauty, we rode horse-back over some of the same trails my father had first cov-ered when he and his brother had hiked in as teenagers. He thought the horses were a big improvement over walking, and so did I.

I enjoyed myself so much, on that trip, that I returned the following year, with a friend and her family. I still steered clear of the cooking and Cindy's mom and grand-mother encouraged me in that — probably having heard about my aversion to cooking. They enthusiastically shooed me toward the glacier streams where I caught my limit of a string of beautiful trout as quickly as I could return my hook to the water. The ice-cold waters of an Oregon glacier lake once again replaced my bath tub.

Although I didn't help with preparing meals, I remember that the food — just like the scenery — was beyond description. You can have croissants in bed at a city hotel but you haven't lived until you wake up under a blue sky pillowed with white clouds to the smell of freshly-brewed coffee, while trout and potatoes sizzled in bacon fat over an open fire. There's nothing like the picture of a string of horses drinking at the edge of a lake catching their reflections in the mirror-like waters along with the peerless azure sky, the snow-capped peaks and the granite covered hills.

I loved to listen to the whispering of the wind rushing through the tall firs. Their limbs move in a trance-like rhythm-back and forth, to and fro, as they have done since the beginning of time. Lying on my back looking up at the dark, star-studded night sky — so close at times and yet so far away, I couldn't help but wonder about "stuff" and "things" that I couldn't put into words.

With an abundance of tourists clamoring for solitude, the wilderness areas of Oregon and Washington are much more in use now than they were when I made my first trip. Disregarding the menace of encroaching civilization, the snow-covered mountain peaks still catch their regal reflection in the crystal blue waters and create the most spectacular scenery imaginable.

I remember my childhood days, and all the unspoken questions I had, and how puzzled I had been by it all. Years later, when I sit quietly at the edge of a silent blue lake tucked against the bottom of a granite-clad mountain, or lie on a blanket under a star-studded night sky, I'm still puzzled and still wonder about "things" and "stuff" and feelings.

Yet, at the same time, in the stillness of the moment, away from cars and telephones, vacuum cleaners and dishwashers, computers and hi-tech calculators, life seems simple, serene and sane.

I did, finally, learn to cook in wilderness camp. I learned to keep it simple and uncluttered, and to be more aware of where I was than what I ate. There's noting tastier than a hamburger patty, a chop or a steak cooked over the open fire — not to mention a freshly-caught brook trout. And nothing surpasses the flavor of a potato wrapped in foil buried beneath the hot coals of the campfire fire for later consumption.

Wilderness Recipes

Wilderness cooking can mean many things. Packing in 40 miles on several horses and mules is much different than hiking 20 miles on foot. I don't know many backpackers who would haul a cast iron skillet on their backs.

The following suggestions are for hikers who want to take the least amount of equipment and supplies. Adventurers accompanied by pack animals have more — but not much more — leeway. I used to return with half the supplies I took, until I had to carry it myself. I have learned to take only what I need.

Breakfast

Granola bars and dried fruits make an easy and nourishing breakfast. (Take along several self-closing plastic food sacks and add some of these to your supplies.)

Birdseed

1 cup toasted sesame seeds

1/3 cup each: hulled sunflower seeds, nuts of your choice, coconut flakes, raisins, toasted wheat germ, mini candy-coated chocolate candies and dried fruit cut into small bits.

Add 1 cup instant dry milk, 1 teaspoon allspice and blend well.

Place 1/2 cup servings into individual plastic sacks. At camp, put mix in bowl and add 1/2 cup cold or hot water and stir.

Mountain Mush

4 cups quick oatmeal
2-1/2 cups mixed seeds and nuts
1 cup shredded coconut
1 cup dried diced fruit
1/2 cup vegetable oil
1/4 cup honey
1/4 cup molasses
1 cup instant dry milk

Mix all ingredients together, spread on cookie sheet. Bake at 275 degrees for about 15 minutes, stirring several times. Continue stirring occasionally as mixture cools.

Store in sealed bags in 1/2 to 3/4 cup portions. At camp, place in bowls and cover with hot water. Let set for several minutes.

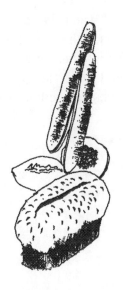

Fruit breads and dense coffee cakes pack well and are good for breakfast, as well as individual pudding cups and fruit rolls. Eggs can be packed in special insulated packs or broken into plastic containers and stuffed in the pack to keep cool. At camp, add freeze-dried meat or salami, cheese and some herbs to scrambled eggs as they cook and serve in pocket bread or on tortillas. Pre-cooked chopped bacon can be carried in a plastic sack for a treat in your breakfast eggs.

Sandwiches, salami, fruit and cheese in strings or pre-cut strips make easy lunches. Try hard rolls, English muffins, cocktail loaves of different types of bread for a change. Margarine or butter flavored with herbs and mayonnaise (herb or mustard flavored) in squeeze-type plastic bottles is a fairly easy accompaniment worth carrying.

A good selection of (expensive) dinner entrees are available at sporting goods stores. Pick up a few meats and try the grocery store for "instant" everything from soup to nuts. Throw two kinds of dried soup mixes together, adding tomato juice instead of water. Pasta is great on the trail if you have access to enough water for cooking. Anything edible you pack is likely to taste great at camp.

Carry some grated parmesan cheese in a shaker — it's a lot lighter than chunks of cheddar. Be sure to take back what you packed in.

A Northwest Gathering of Nuts

They made little rafts out of twigs and they paddled away
over the water to Owl Island to gather nuts.
Each squirrel had a little sack and a large oar, and spread
out his tail for a sail.
Beatrix Potter - Squirrel Nutkin

The countryside in the fall may not have the startling display of color of a New England autumn, but just the same, the Northwest turns into an incredibly lovely tapestry of golds, shades of red, hanging-in-there summer green offset by the darker hues of the evergreens. The fields have been harvested, the rich, dark earth lies shrouded in the mist of a fall day. When the sun breaks through, the rolling hillsides come alive in their salute to another season.

Sarah is back in school and whenever I find myself free to do as I please, I'm out there roaming the countryside looking for — nuts!

You would think that after all the berries, fruits and vegetables have been harvested, dried, canned, frozen and stored, that life for the Northwestern gatherer is over. Not so! You believe that all my nooks and crannies are over-flowing. Wrong. I'll make room for more.

Walnut and filbert orchards, big and small, offer the fruits of their labors around October — along with some generous backyard nut growers who appear at my door with grocery bags full of nuts from the overflow of their own har-vest. (Did you know that Oregon grows 10 percent of the world's demand for filberts?)

I came across a country store in Dundee, in the heart of nut country, where among other foods, two square wooden bins brimming over with walnuts and filberts stood side by side next to a small box of mixed nuts. I was check-ing out the big bin of filberts, when to the sounds of delighted gasps and surprised chuckles from the customers in the store, a squirrel family marched in — mother, father, two kids — looked neither left nor right and headed straight for the box of mixed nuts. Gracefully raising themselves on their haunches, they dipped in, filled their cheeks to burst-ing with nuts, and unhurriedly departed the store through the open front door from where they had entered.

The owner of the store, with a big grin on his face, explained that those "customers" of his had been around for several seasons. Somehow he had trained them to help themselves only from the one special container of mixed nuts, never touching the big bins. Smart shoppers!

The same Saturday markets, roadside stands and hand-painted signs at country lanes that lead to the farmer's barn I frequented at the end of summer, now offer walnuts and hazelnuts — in the shell or out. I immediately think of the holidays, and baking, and candy-making and gift-giving and buy more than my share of fragrant dark filberts and

shelled walnuts that have never seen the inside of a processing plant or the bins of a glossy supermarket.

After I've sorted through my nut treasures, I placed
them in plastic baggies, sealed tightly, and stored my horde
in the freezer. They'll keep fresh until the next season rolls
around — unless of course, a family of squirrels find them
first.

Between work, keeping house, being with Sarah,
reading everything I can lay my hands on — not to mention
writing — I find myself in the kitchen doing "recreational"
cooking. There is something utterly soul-satisfying in going
through my collection of family recipes, making up my
own, preparing something delicious and having my family
enjoy it. Being raised on a farm has not only given me
appreciation for the hard work it takes to grow and care for
the land, but it has instilled in me a delight in using nature's
bounty and sharing it with family and friends. Everything
tastes better in good company.

This nutty nibbles recipe is one everybody enjoys and
has earned far more compliments than it takes time to fix.

Microwave Nut Nibbles

2 cups shelled walnuts
1/2 cup sugar
3 tablespoons butter
1/2 teaspoon all spice
1/4 cup brandy, bourbon, or rum

In a microwave-proof pie dish soak nuts in brandy for one hour (or more), turning them occasionally to coat them with brandy.

Add all other ingredients; place in microwave for 4 minutes on high. Stir nuts well. Microwave 5 more times for 1 minute each, stirring after each cooking. Place nuts on foil to dry and cool. Store in airtight container. DELICIOUS!

Pack them in attractive glass jars or decorated tins for gifts.

Filbert Tips

For a touch of Oregon, roast a handful of shelled filberts until golden, crumble into bits, and sprinkle over a tossed green salad with a vinegarette dressing.

For a change in flavors substitute filberts for walnuts in cookie and cake recipes. You will delight in the result.

Herb-o-Mania! Parsley, Sage, Rosemary and Thyme

Anything green that grew out of the mould,
Was an excellent herb to our fathers of Old.
Rudyard Kipling

There was a time when herbs belonged to the past — mysterious plants and things witch doctors carried around in dried gourds or greasy leather pouches. Great-grandmothers recommended herbal teas for tummy aches and the chills — long before penicillin and ultra sound. I grew up with steaming cups of pale golden "mountain tea" which was quickly administered whenever I was viewed as looking a bit pale or I dared to sneeze. Peppermint tea was another remedy my family swore by. I still do.

Of course modern medicine came along and made little of things that grew in the earth and synthetic miracle cures were born in steel and chrome laboratories. But things being what they are, and the fact that change is permanent, herbs have risen to a place of importance not only in the preparation of food, but in promising us a healthier life. The planet has become a Garden of Eden for herb lovers. Today, people grow herb gardens in their back yards, next to the flower garden; between bricks on walks, on the back decks of their houseboats, in huge clay pots on patios, balconies, roof gardens and window sills.

No respectable cook would dare live without a herb garden — the smallest one I've ever had was on my window sill where sweet basil thrived happily alongside of parsley, oregano and cilantro and the ever faithful, hard-to-kill pot of chives. Also, flavoring dishes with herbs eliminates the use of salt in many instances.

Sweet basil, oregano and cilantro have become household words. Parsley, sage, rosemary and thyme, are not just part of a song, but lend character to fish, fowl and roast alike. My herbalist friend tells me that echinacia helps protect and strengthen the immune system, that dandelion is high in minerals and acts as a diuretic, while valerian is supposed to calm body and spirit. Now that's what I call back to basics. Who knows, we may just have over-medicated ourselves and made the pharmaceutical industry into the monstrous giant it has become.

Herb farms are part of the Northwest scenery, and some of them are quite lavish and diversified. Besides growing herbs in flats and pots for sale, their owners have added gift stores, countrified and charmingly intimate dining rooms where herb-laden meals are served at lunch and dinner time, and where chefs offer classes in cooking with herbs to anyone willing to sign up.

Farm stores are usually filled with cleverly designed gift baskets, wreaths made of dried laurel leaves, garlic heads and fiery red peppers — and it all smells heavenly. I recently plowed through an array of herb-filled pots in a small herb farm near the Oregon coast and left with several small containers of tender green things sprouting and a wealth of information on how to care for them.

I have come up with some of my own ways for cooking with herbs and to my delight both my family and my friends loved it. I'm sure these recipes will add new vigor and interest to your dinner table.

Pesto for Pasta and More

Pesto

> 1/2 cup olive oil
> 1 cup sweet basil, chopped fine
> 2 cloves garlic, finely chopped

Pasta PrimaVera

In 1 cup of olive oil marinate for at least 6 hours:
2 large, seeded and diced tomatoes
4 ounces chopped brie
1/2 cup finely chopped fresh basil

In your favorite pasta pot cook 1 pound (serves four people) fresh linguini or fettuccini al dente, drain in colander, return to still hot pasta pot and toss with olive mixture.

This is the base recipe; you can add other chopped vegetables of your choice. I prefer snap peas, green peas and tiny buds of broccoli.

Garlic Points

Prepare your usual mixture of butter and garlic, add 1 tablespoon fresh (or 1 teaspoon dried) basil, a good pinch of rosemary, plus 1/2 tsp. fennel seeds.

Thinly slice a baguette of French bread, dip quickly into hot butter-garlic-basil melt, transfer to cooky sheet, bake at 375 till crisp and golden! (Will keep in air tight container for two to three weeks.)

Herb Tips

Add 1 tsp. rosemary to roasting potatoes and vegetables. Delicious.

Use rosemary in lamb and pot roasts.

Make pockets in leg of lamb and stuff with slivers of garlic.

A Touch of Garlic — A Taste of Onion

Eat no onions nor garlic, for we are to utter sweet breath.
Shakespeare
A Midsummer-Night's Dream

Even though Shakespeare may have been responsible for our usage of the words "garlic mouth" and "onion breath" as a sort of humorous insult and a less-than-funny ethnic slur, I can't imagine cooking without either one of these flavor-giving bulbs.

Those little cloves that nestle spoon-like in silk-thin skins forming a cluster wrapped in a final layer of filmy tissue have been around as long as the ages, and have added their flavor to food prepared by cavemen and haughty French chefs alike.

Garlic has been attributed with healing powers, a source for preventing illness and is, according to some people, the cure-all for major health problems. But more than that, garlic is to cooking what toe shoes are to dancing. Just where do you think "Alfredo" would be without a clove or two or three? And no matter how *"al dente'* the linguini primavera may be, without garlic this popular dish would be banished for eternity from the tables of Rome.

There is an annual garlic festival in Oregon where garlic enthusiasts demonstrate their ideas for using garlic in everything short of garlic toothpaste and perfume. Driving to the country town where the festival is held, I just follow my nose for the last two miles — never mind the signs — park the car and head for the stands and tents where garlic is king and where giant elephant garlic, to midget-size pearl-like bulbs, wreaths, braids and garlic pyramids all vie for attention. Garlic afficionados are nice people and are they ever dedicated. You'd have to be garlic-crazy to use garlic the way they do!

A garlic festival is like a specialty farmer's market. Garlic lovers bathed in clouds of the bulb's unmistakable aroma offer their wares from behind stands, tents and tail-gates. By the time I'm ready to leave, I have ended up with a braided tail of garlic heads — both for decorative and edible purposes — several recipes that would earn any cook a medal for bravery, a white ceramic pot with vents for stor-ing it, a garlic roaster and a garlic mouth from tasting my way through the festival.

The event took place on a warm and sunny Northwest late summer Sunday too lovely to stay indoors. And, if garlic was the reason that brought me out of the house, it is probably as powerful as "they" say it is.

For a real treat, for something different, try roasted garlic accompanied by a hunk of warm brie as an appetizer served with thin rounds of French bread. Even if it sounds foreboding, be brave and try the sealed clay-pot garlic chicken dinner — it's delicious.

Baked Garlic

2 heads of garlic (not pealed or separated)
Olive oil

Rub garlic generously with olive oil. Bake in 350 oven until skin splits and cloves pop up; about 20 minutes, or microwave on high about 6 minutes.

Heat 6 ounces brie in microwave for 1 minute.

Clay Pot Baked Garlic Chicken

1 cut-up fryer chicken or
6 split-halves chicken breasts
6 heads of garlic
1 bouquet garni
1/2 cup flour - water

Make a thick paste with flour and water; set aside.

Soak clay pot in water according to instructions.

Place chicken pieces, garlic and bouquet garni in clay-pot.

Apply flour paste to the edges of the bottom part of the clay pot, fit lid tightly over bottom of pot to seal air tight.

Bake at 375 degrees for 1 hour.

Break flour seal, remove lid, place under broiler long enough to evenly brown chicken.

Serve with your favorite side dishes.

(Remember, once garlic and onions have been stewed, cooked, roasted or baked for any length of time, they lose their strong odor and leave just a touch of their flavor.)

Let onion atoms lurk within the bowl,
And half suspected,
Animate the whole.

Lady Holland's Memoir

And when it comes to onions, well, I believe I have chopped more onions in my life than anything else that comes across my chopping block. As a girl, I remember peeling my very first onion with tears in my eyes and the sharp sting of its many layers irritating my nose. Finally a kind soul told me that if held the peeled onion under cold running water, chopping would be less annoying. It worked!

Driving around the Northwest and coming across acres after acres of onion fields, I realize that regardless of their nasty attacks on tear ducts and nostrils, the whole world is waiting for the next onion harvest. From the state of Washington come the world famous Walla Walla Sweets, which try to outdo the everyday garden variety of plain, old, golden onions. I guess to some people, an onion is an onion — Walla Walla or not!

There is hardly a main dish that doesn't call for an onion — yellow or red — or one of its chic relatives: scallions, leeks, chives and shallots. I love them all! For a special dish that's quite different, onion lovers — try it; you'll like it. (It goes with all your meat dishes, or can be a meal by itself.)

Onion Lover's Pie

Use prepared pie crust, or make crust from your favorite pie crust recipe and transfer to an 11-inch tart or pie pan. Line crust with foil, fill with pie weights or dried beans and bake at 425 for 15 minutes. Remove weights and foil, continue to bake for 10 minutes. Cool.

Filling
1/2 stick butter
1-3/4 pounds onions, sliced thin
1 cup half and half
1 egg plus 3 yolks
4 ounce Fontina cheese, grated
Dash of nutmeg
Salt and pepper to taste

Melt butter, saute onions over medium-low heat until soft and golden, about 45 minutes, stirring occasionally. Let cool to room temperature. Whisk half and half, nutmeg, egg and yolks; season sparingly with salt and pepper. Spread onions in crust, sprinkle with grated cheese, add half and half mixture.

Bake tart at 325 until filling puffs up and is golden, about 50 minutes. Cool slightly. Serve warm.

A Jug of Wine

Drink no longer water,
But use a little wine for your stomach's sake.
Corinthians

There must be a million sayings praising the virtues of wine. Odes have been written touting the color and the flavor of this heady nectar. Connoisseurs know all about good years and vintage values, and tasters roll and swish the liquid expertly around in their mouths and sniff the cork for answers to unwritten questions. They can pronounce Chateau La Tour, Champagne de Moet and Piesporter Goldtroepfchen with the same ease I read Mother Goose stories.

Well, I don't know much about wine — just enough to know the difference between "Ripple" and Chardonnay, and to enjoy it. I guess the poets were right. A glass of ruby-red Northwest wine glowing in a goblet, or shades of pale gold liquid shimmering in slim stemware lends a festive air to the dinner table and a make a simple meal a celebration. A toast to one's health, a toast to a New Year or a toast to newly-weds is indeed a toast to the tradition of well-wishing. And, it's done with a glass of wine. I love tradition.

Many people have traded in their well-stocked liquor cabinets for a simple wine rack and have become collectors of certain wines. They know how and when to turn a bottle and what year was "A Wine Year" for what grape. They have the proper glasses without chips at the rim or stem, and they don't really care what they drink as long as they pronounce it right.

Me, well, I just drink it, save the corks, glue them together and make great hot pads out of them. I love champagne as well — paint the corks gold and silver and turn them into Christmas tree ornaments. See what you can do if you drink enough wine?

The Northwest has earned its share of kudos for growing award-winning wines on sloping hillsides where the soil and the weather are perfect. Our wines compare more than favorably with its foreign relatives — and we are proud of them. After the garlic festivals, an Octoberfest and Christmas crafts fairs, a wine-tasting event draws me like a grape draws sunshine.

Each year wine tastings are happening all summer long all over the Northwest, and these events are usually well attended. Let's face it. It's one big party where vintners display the products of their vineyards with paternal pride and pleasure under banners and backdrops that advertise the name of their enterprise. They handle bottles of their wine with the same care I hold a baby, before they ceremoniously uncork a bottle and pour a generous sip into a small wine glass and offer a taste, along with a delicious nibble or two. Taste enough, drink enough and I guarantee you walk out with a case! But that's all right. After all, what you don't drink you'll use for cooking.

I firmly believe that a glass or two of wine cannot only enhance a meal, but does wonders when used in preparing even the simplest dishes. I love to cook with wine and have turned many a mediocre main course into a lip-smacking dish. Add one cup of a robust, red wine to any pot roast, a cut of venison, a lowly batch of beef stew, roast duck or pheasant, and your meal becomes "gourmet."

Whenever an amount of water is recommended for a light sauce for fish or chicken, I substitute a dry white wine. I steam my clams and mussels in a mixture of half white wine, half water, a clove of garlic, a stem of celery, a small tomato, a slice of onion and a sprig of fennel green.

Try it — like the Bible says, "Use a little wine for your health!"

Fireside Warm Mulled Wine

For Blustery Evenings and Other Celebrations

2 bottles of a light red wine
2 oranges
8 orange slices
1-1/2 cups water
1 cup Sugar
24 whole cloves
5 cinnamon sticks

Cut oranges in quarters and stud with 3 cloves each. In a non-aluminum pot bring water to boil, add sugar, cinnamon sticks, sugar and quartered oranges. Stir until sugar dissolves. Simmer over medium heat for 6 minutes Add wine, simmer (do not let boil) on low heat for 10 minutes. Remove orange pieces and cinnamon sticks. Pour into mugs and garnish with additional cinnamon sticks and attach orange slices to rim of mug.

A Patchwork Quilt Of This and That ... And Baking Bread

"Give us this day our daily bread ..."

The Northwest has not lost its rural charm altogether, because people have taken care to preserve some traditions and have gracefully combined city life with country ways. Rural life with its simple pleasures hovers at the edges of even our major cities. I don't have a farm but I get my farm-fresh eggs from Lynn, a neighbor, who lives a couple of miles down the road from my house. I usually stop by a little early on egg day, before the eggs have been gathered. Then I get to walk around the barnyard where chickens, horses, dogs and cats coexist in peaceful harmony next to a motorhome.

I'm a farm girl at heart, and I am very much at home in the barnyard. I like to wander through the barn where the sweet smell of straw and hay mingle with the distinct fragrance of a new apple harvest stored in wooden bins to last through the winter. Bundles of Lynn's dried "everlasting" flowers, their colors muted, hang from the rafters in orderly rows. The three assorted barn kittens Lynn's family rescued from a ditch, roll playfully on their backs, paw the air and attack my shoe laces. Unconcerned with the kittens or the pecking, cackling chickens and wing-flapping roosters, Candy, the family dog runs to me with her old, grey tennis ball clamped securely in her teeth, drops the ball and barks sharply demanding my attention.

Everybody gets along with everybody, and I wonder why people can't practice a little bit of barnyard policy, not to mention harmony — or at least be a lot more diplomatic about co-existence than they are now. There's nothing wrong with learning about life from the critters. They have an admirable dignity and sense of order all of their own. We all could use a good dose of that.

With the exception of the telephone extension in the barn and the sleek motorhome for fast get-aways, Lynn's barnyard is no different from the one my great-grandparents had on their farm.

It was there, the story goes, that my great grandmother and her sister were entertaining themselves while their parents went to town for supplies. The enterprising youngsters decided to experiment with tying the tails of two calves together. Of course as soon as the kids accomplished their deed and released the calves from their restraining hold, the frightened little beasts took off in opposite directions. To make matters worse, they bucked and strained against each other in vain to free themselves and only succeeded in tightening their loosely looped tails into an iron knot.

The children were hysterical. One of the girls headed for the house to get a butcher knife to slice through the knot before the folks returned from their trip to town. However, my grandma's aunt, nine-year old Becky, couldn't stand to to see the calves' tails get butchered. She saved the day by untying the knot — with her teeth — while her cohorts kept a tight grip on the scared critters — quite a feat at that! Relieved, calves and kids scattered in all directions, and no one was the wiser.

Stories like that coupled with my memory of growing up on a farm among lots of family are never far from instant recall. Whenever I bake bread in my citified kitchen, I always think back to the time when my mother's watchful eye followed me as I trotted through the tall pasture grass on my way to my grandmother's house where I watched Nita bake bread. Since the kitchen counters were the low, old-fashioned kind, I could easily observe as Nita folded, punched, turned and shaped a big ball of dough into smooth, satiny loaves.

If I behaved long enough, I was rewarded with a slice of warm-from-the-oven bread loaded with butter and heaped high with delicious jam. I still remember the old farm kitchen, the cupboards filled with Grandma's favorite Desert Rose dishes, and the Dilly Bar treats straight from the Dairy Queen that were stored in the big freezer on the back porch.

Years later I tried baking bread, but my first attempts didn't yield the kind of picture-perfect loaves that came from Nita's flour-covered hands. But practice makes perfect, I overcame the fear of flour, and my bread baking projects passed inspection. Though bread machines litter department stores and kitchen boutiques, and jump at you from the pages of state-of-the art gadgetry catalogues, I find great satisfaction in kneading, pounding and punching my own dough the old-fashioned way.

The bread recipes (in the recipe section) are easy enough for even the novice. Don't let fear of flour stop you from enjoying the delicious, mouth watering flavors and heart warming aroma of home-baked bread.

After-Thoughts

I like living.
I have sometimes been wildly, despairingly, acutely miser-
able, racked with sorrow,
But through it all I still know quite certainly that just to be
alive is a grand thing.
Agatha Christie

When Abigail Scott was seventeen, she helped her mother hide a set of six Dutch dinner plates in a feather bed to take with them on the long journey from Illinois to Oregon. She also smuggled in a spelling book, because she felt words were priceless and with them you could do anything.

The following year, Abigail married young Ben Duniway and began a life of pioneer drudgery — she made thousands of pounds of butter to sell at market, she baked and cleaned and stewed and fried and raised kids and carried water and split wood and nursed sick children. She also wrote poetry and stories about farm life and sold them to territory newspapers, and penned fiery replies to the acerbic male commentary about "women's place" being in the home.

In 1859 Oregon became a state and Abigail Scott Duniway wrote the first novel to be published west of the Rocky Mountains. She later called the book an indiscretion, saying she outgrew it before it reached the public eye. However, Abigail's fame far outshone that of her book. She helped start the fight for women's suffrage and the right to vote in the west. After a forty-one year struggle, she became the first woman in Oregon to cast a ballot.

When I decided to write a book, I had no idea how complicated and frustrating an undertaking it would be. "Writing is very easy," an author once stated, "all you have to do is sit staring at a blank page until drops of blood form on your forehead." I haven't noticed any blood yet, but it was much harder to put on paper how I felt about everything — my family, food, the Northwest and myself, than it ever was to cook a dinner — even a dinner for fifty.

However, as blank pieces of paper slowly began filling up with thoughts and musings and recollections, as I transferred to paper recipes straight from my kitchen, and the pages grew into a respectable stack — my terror subsided, and I realized how much this process of writing has meant to me. I realize how precious those memories of my home, my family and my friends are. I began to understand that putting it all down on paper, committing my appreciation and enjoyment to print is in itself an act of love.

I have learned a lot more about patience and kindness and the value of family ties and friendship bonds. I have learned that being alone is fine, but that the support from the people in my life has provided me with an inexplicable sense of comfort and an awareness of truly being loved. Like Abigail, I have changed and I guess I will do a lot more changing as I keep on growing, and reaching and stretching, like a sapling in the midst of tall and mighty firs.

I am fortunate. I live in a place where in spite of the turmoil and the overwhelming pain in the world, there is a measure of peace and serenity; where the ocean dwarfs my importance and gives me a sense of divine reality. When I walk the land, when I look at the wheat fields and the corn fields rich and ready with harvest, when I hear the laughter of kids sailing through the air on a rope swing tied to an old tree in the yard, when I come into my kitchen to the satisfying smells of simple, good cooking, I know I belong. And that feels good!

Cooking is like love.
It should be entered into with
abandon or not at all.

Harriet Van Horne

One Dish Meals and Potluck Fare

Sheepherder Spuds

4 potatoes, scrubbed and
  chopped or leftovers,
  already cooked
6 slices bacon, chopped and
  fried

1 small onion, chopped fine
3 or 4 eggs, slightly scrambled

1. If your potatoes are already cooked, fry them in 2 tablespoons of oil for about 8 minutes, or until they start to brown. If the spuds are raw, they'll need more oil and more time — about 15 minutes.
2. Add the onion and cook, stirring, until it is no longer crunchy. Then add the bacon pieces and the eggs and cook, stirring, until the eggs are thoroughly done.
3. Serve with toast, and put the ketchup bottle on the table if you like it on French fries.

Buckaroo Beans

2 cups pinto beans
6 cups cold water
1 to 2 onions chopped
2 big garlic cloves chopped or
  mashed
1 small bay leaf
1/2 pound smoked ham
2 cups canned tomatoes

1/2 cup green pepper, chopped
2 teaspoons chile powder
2 tablespoons brown sugar
1/2 teaspoon dry mustard
1/4 teaspoon oregano or
  cumin
Salt to taste.

1. Wash the pinto beans and soak overnight in cold water.
2. Add onions, garlic, bay leaf and ham. Bring to boil rapidly. Reduce heat and simmer, covered tightly, for 1-1/2 hours.
3. Add other ingredients, cook for 30 minutes.

Ham Loaf

1 pound smoked ham, no fat,
  ground
3/4 pound lean ground beef
1/4 pound fresh pork ground
  or mild sausage

2 eggs
3/4 cup fine dry bread crumbs
1-1/2 cups tomato juice,
  divided
Sprinkle of pepper

1. To ground meats add the eggs, bread crumbs, pepper and 3/4 cup tomato juice. Form into a loaf.
2. Bake in a 325 degree oven for 45 minutes.
3. Pour 3/4 cup tomato juice over the loaf and bake 45 minutes longer.

Serves five or six.

Cindy's Chicken Enchiladas

1 large onion, sliced
3/4 pound mushrooms, sliced
1 cup margarine
1 can (4 ounces) chopped
  chilies, drained
2 cups chopped olives
1 chicken, cooked, boned and
  diced

4 ounces cream cheese
1 package 12" tortillas
1-1/2 pound jack cheese,
  shredded
1 cup whipping cream.

1. In sauce pan saute onion and mushrooms in margarine until limp.
2. Add chilies, olives and chicken, heat and blend.
3. Put cream cheese on top of mixture, cover and heat.
4. Fry tortillas in hot oil to blister. Stuff generously with chicken mixture and place in 9" x 13" casserole. Cover with shredded cheese, then pour cream over.
5. Bake at 350 degrees for 20 minutes to melt cheese and blend in cream.

Serves eight.
Freezes well.
Better the second day.

Don't let mike (uncle mike?!) get near the batch in progress :)

Joan

Chicken with Forty Cloves of Garlic

2/3 cup vegetable oil
8 chicken legs and 8 thighs
4 ribs celery, cut in long strips
2 medium onions, chopped
6 sprigs parsley
1 tablespoon fresh tarragon,
  chopped (or 1 teaspoon
  dried)

1/2 cup dry vermouth
2-1/2 teaspoons salt
1/4 teaspoon freshly ground
  black pepper
Generous dash nutmeg, grated
40 cloves garlic, unpeeled.

1. Put the oil in a shallow dish: add the chicken pieces, coat with oil.

2. Cover the bottom of a heavy 6-quart casserole with the celery and onion. Add parsley and tarragon and lay the chicken pieces on top.

3. Pour vermouth over all. Sprinkle with salt, pepper and nutmeg. Tuck garlic around and between the chicken pieces.

4. Cover the top of the casserole tightly with aluminum foil, then the lid (this creates an airtight seal so the steam does not escape).

5. Bake at 350 degrees for 1-1/2 hours without removing the cover.

6. Serve the chicken, pan juices and whole garlic cloves with thin slices of heated French bread or hot toast. The garlic should be squeezed from the root end of its papery husk onto the bread or toast, spread like butter and eaten with the chicken.

Serves eight.

Frijoles Borrachos (Drunken Beans)

4 cups pinto beans
1 tablespoon soda
2 chopped onions
2 cloves garlic, chopped
4 slices bacon
1 tablespoon salt

1/2 teaspoon sugar
1 can beer
2 tablespoons chili powder,
   optional
1 tablespoon cumin
1 teaspoon oregano

1. Soak beans overnight. Drain, discard floaters.
2. Cover with fresh water, bring to boil. Boil for 15 minutes.
3. Add soda, stir until foamy. Drain and rinse.
4. Cover with fresh water. Add onions, garlic and bacon and cook for 3-1/2 hours.
5. Add the rest of the ingredients and cook for 30 minutes.

Serves eight.

Chicken Piccata

1-1/2 pounds chicken breasts, boned and skinned, pounded thin and cut into 3-inch pieces.
1/2 cup flour
1/2 teaspoon salt
1/4 teaspoon white pepper
1/2 cup butter or half oil, half butter

1/2 cup chicken stock
1 cup dry, white wine
2 tablespoons capers, rinsed and drained
Fresh ground pepper
1/4 teaspoon salt
1 lemon, sliced thin
1 tablespoon parsley, minced
4 cups cooked rice

1. Place flour, salt and white pepper in a shallow dish and mix well. Dip each piece of chicken in flour and place on another plate.

2. Heat 2 tablespoons butter in a heavy skillet over medium heat. Saute the chicken quickly a few pieces at a time, using about 1 tablespoons butter at a time. Remove the sauteed chicken to a warm platter and keep covered.

3. Pour the chicken stock into the pan drippings. Simmer gently, stirring up the brown bits with a wooden spoon. Add wine and salt and simmer 2 minutes.

4. Return chicken to skillet and simmer covered 2 to 3 minutes until bubbly. Sprinkle with fresh ground pepper and the capers.

5. Arrange the chicken on the rice on a large platter. Pour the sauce over the chicken and garnish with the lemon slices and parsley.

Serves six.

Onion Soup

4 large onions, sliced thin
1/2 cup butter
4 cans chicken broth (13-1/2 ounce cans)
1 cup dry white wine (optional)

1/8 teaspoon marjoram leaves, crushed
1/4 cup parmesan cheese, shredded

1. Saute onions in butter until soft. Add other ingredients simmer 15 minutes.
2. Serve with French bread slices and parmesan cheese on top.

Pasta, Pasta

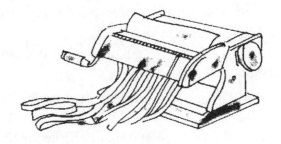

Japanese Salad

Salad
1 package ramen noodles, crushed
2 tablespoons toasted sesame seeds
1 tablespoon margarine
1 head lettuce or cabbage, chopped fine
6 green onions, sliced

Dressing
2 tablespoons sugar
1 tablespoon monosodium glutamate
1/4 cup vinegar
1/4 cup salad oil
2 drops sesame oil
Salt and pepper to taste

1. Fry noodles in margarine until golden, add seeds, toss and drain on paper towel.
2. Mix lettuce or cabbage and onions in salad bowl.
3. Top with dressing.
4. Toss noodles and seeds over salad at last minute.

For variety mix 1 can shrimp or chicken with lettuce and onions. You may sprinkle chopped almonds over the top for a slightly different taste.

This recipe has been around for about two decades but it still interests almost everybody who tastes it at my table. Infinitely variable, it is a good standby salad.

Sesame Rice Noodles

4 ounces rice vermicelli
Hot water
1-1/2 tablespoons Oriental
   sesame oil
1 teaspoon chili oil, or
   crushed red pepper flakes to
   taste

3 green onions, cut into slivers
1/2 red bell pepper, seeded,
   cut into paper-thin slivers
1 cup fresh bean sprouts
1/4 cup fresh cilantro, minced
Salt to taste.

1. Put vermicelli in a large bowl and cover with hot tap water. Soak until soft, 10 minutes, then drain.
2. Heat both oils in a wok or large skillet over high heat. When oil is hot, add noodles, stir well and cook 45 seconds. Add onions, bell pepper, sprouts, cilantro and salt. Cook and stir 30 seconds.
3. Remove from heat and serve hot or at room temperature.

Pasta Port Umatilla

1 pound bow tie (farfalle) pasta
1 medium red onion, sliced
1 large red bell pepper, seeded and sliced
1/4 cup olive oil
3/4 cup plain black olives
1-1/2 cups crumbled feta cheese
1 large jar marinated artichoke hearts, cut in chunks
1/4 cup marinade from artichoke hearts
1 large lemon, juiced
Pepper, freshly ground
Salt
Parsley to garnish

1. Cook pasta in boiling, salted water.
2. Lightly saute onion and red pepper in olive oil.
3. Rinse pasta in hot water and return to medium heat. Toss over heat with onion, pepper, cheese, olives, artichoke hearts and marinade.
4. When thoroughly tossed and heated through, remove from heat and add lemon juice, pepper and salt to taste. Garnish with parsley and serve in heated serving dish, warm.

White Beans and Pasta

12 slices bacon, chopped (or more to taste)
1 large onion, chopped
16 ounces tomato sauce
2 cups cooked white beans
Basil to taste

Garlic to taste
1 pound elbow, shell or twist macaroni, cooked and drained
3/4 cup Jack cheese, shredded

1. Brown bacon. Drain, set aside.
2. In bacon grease, saute onion until limp. Drain off fat. Add tomato sauce, beans and seasonings. Cook down, about 20 minutes to reduce liquid and blend seasonings.
3. Pour pasta onto large, warm serving platter or baking pan. Cover with sauce, then bacon and top with cheese. Broil briefly to melt cheese.

Shrimp and Veggie Linguini

1 pound fresh linguini
1 pound large shrimp, cooked
3/4 pound mushrooms, sliced
3 large shallots, sliced fine
2 cloves garlic, sliced
2 large tomatoes, seeded and diced
1 package snap peas, thawed and drained
1/3 cup plus 4 tablespoons olive oil
2 ounces brie, diced
4 tablespoons capers (optional)
1/2 cup dry, white wine
1/4 cup heavy cream
4 tablespoons fresh basil, chopped
Salt and pepper to taste (optional)
Parmesan cheese for serving

1. Soak brie, tomatoes and basil in 1/3 cup olive oil over night.

2. Saute garlic, shallots and mushrooms till semi-tender in 4 tablespoons olive oil (about 8 minutes). Add wine, cook till liquid reduced to half. Put aside.

3. Cook linguini and drain. Return to hot pan on low heat. Add shrimp, seasoning, tomato-brie-basil mixture and toss. Add mushroom-shallot-wine mixture, stir constantly till all ingredients are heated through. Do not let boil.

4. Add cream, blend. Sprinkle with parmesan and serve.

Serves six.
Delicious!

Northwest Clam Sauce Linguini

1 pound fresh linguini
1 pound fresh steamer clams
4 tablespoons olive oil
2 green bell peppers, chopped
4 cloves garlic, chopped fine
1/2 pound fresh mushrooms,
  sliced

1/2 cup dry, white wine
2 tablespoons cornstarch
Salt and pepper to taste
  (optional)
4 cans (6-1/2 ounce) chopped
  clams (do not drain)
1 cup parmesan for table

1. Saute onion, garlic, green peppers and mushrooms in olive oil for 8 minutes. Reduce heat, add wine, seasoning, and chopped clams. Let come to a boil, remove from heat. (The sauce can be prepared 3 days ahead, refrigerated and reheated.)

2. Steam clams in boiling water till shells open. Do not serve clams that remain closed during steaming process.

3. Cook linguini al dente. Place in large (warm) serving platter or bowl, top with sauce, circle with steamed clams. Serve with parmesan and garlic points.

Serves six.

Seafood

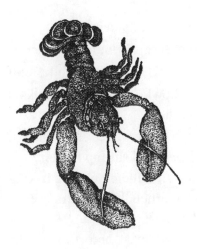

Tillamook Bay Cheese Bake

1 pound Monterey Jack
cheese, grated
1 pound medium cheddar
cheese, grated
6 eggs separated
1/2 pound fresh bay shrimp
6 to 8 canned artichoke hearts,
quartered
1/4 cup green onion, chopped

1 cup evaporated milk, undiluted, or half and half
2 tablespoons flour
1/2 teaspoon black pepper
1/2 teaspoon salt
1/4 teaspoon basil
2 to 3 medium tomatoes,
sliced

1. Preheat oven to 325 degrees.

2. Combine cheese, shrimp and green onions.

3. In another bowl, beat eggs whites until stiff.

4. In another bowl, combine egg yolks, milk, flour, salt, pepper and basil.

5. Fold beaten eggs whites into egg yolk mixture, then fold in cheese and shrimp mixture.

6. Turn into well-buttered oblong baking dish (12" x 8") and arrange artichoke quarters evenly over the casserole. Bake for 30 minutes.

7. Remove from oven and arrange the tomato slices, overlapping slightly, over top of casserole. Bake an additional 15 to 20 minutes, until set.

8. Cool a few minutes before cutting into squares. Serve.

Sole Fillets with an Extra Touch

6 fillets of sole (one for each
   serving)
Cracker meal
Oil or bacon grease to cover
   frying pan bottom
Salt to taste

1/4 teaspoon paprika
1/4 cube butter or margarine
1/2 cup green onions, chopped
1/2 cup green olives with
   pimento, sliced
1/2 cup vermouth

1. Pat fillets dry on paper towel. Coat with cracker meal.
2. Melt bacon grease or heat oil in frying pan until bubbling.
3. Salt fillets and sprinkle with paprika. Place in pan and fry 5 minutes on each side. Take out of pan and place in baking dish.
4. In the pan melt butter, add onions and olives. Add vermouth and blend well. Pour over the fillets.
5. Bake in 350 degree oven for 20 minutes.

Halibut with Almond Butter

1/2 cup unsalted butter
3-1/2 ounces sliced or slivered
   almonds
2 to 3 tablespoons lemon juice
Dash Worcestershire sauce

1 tablespoons minced parsley
4 halibut steaks or fillets
   (about 1-1/2 pounds fish)
Parsley sprigs (for garnish)

1. Preheat broiler.
2. In a small frying pan over medium heat, melt 1/4 cup of butter until foamy and light brown. Add almonds and saute until lightly toasted.
3. Place all but a few almonds in blender or food processor. Add lemon juice, Worcestershire sauce, remaining butter in pieces, and half the minced parsley. Blend or process 10 seconds. Remove from container and chill.
4. Broil halibut 4 inches from heat until first side is lightly browned (3 to 5 minutes). Turn and broil until fish flakes easily at the touch of a fork (3 to 5 minutes more).
5. Dollop 2 tablespoons almond butter on each steak. Sprinkle with reserved almonds and minced parsley. Garnish with parsley sprigs.

Pesto Rotini and Shrimp

1 pound rotini pasta
1/2 to 1 pound cooked small
  shrimp
2 cups shredded red cabbage,
  about 1/2 small cabbage

1/4 cup plus 2 tablespoons
  commercial or homemade
  pesto sauce
1/2 cup oil-and-vinegar dressing or vinaigrette

1. Cook pasta in a large pot of boiling water, al dente, about 10 minutes. Drain and rinse under cold water.

2. Place pasta in a bowl with shrimp and cabbage.

3. Whisk 1/4 cup pesto into vinaigrette or dressing. Toss with pasta. Taste and add another 2 tablespoons pesto if needed.

4. Serve immediately or refrigerate.

Serves four to six.

Wild Rice and Shrimp

2/3 cup uncooked wild rice
2 cups water
1/2 teaspoon salt
1 cup chopped green pepper
1 cup chopped celery
1/2 cup chopped green onion
1 clove garlic finely chopped
1/4 cup olive or vegetable oil

1 can tomato sauce (8 ounces)
1 cup water
1 teaspoon salt
1/2 teaspoon oregano ground
1/2 teaspoon basil ground
1/4 teaspoon seasoned pepper
1 pound cooked shrimp

1. Wash and drain rice. Heat rice, water and salt to boil. Reduce heat, cover and simmer until tender, about 45 minutes. Drain.

2. Saute pepper, celery, onion and garlic in oil. Add tomato sauce, water and seasoning. Heat to boil. Simmer 10 minutes uncovered. Stir in shrimp.

3. Place rice in a 2-quart casserole, add shrimp mix, toss gently.

4. Bake at 350 degrees for 30 minutes.

Yaquina Crab Cakes

1/2 stick butter
1/2 teaspoon flour
3/4 cup cream
1-1/2 pounds lump crabmeat
3 slices bread, crumbled
1 tablespoon mayonnaise

Salt to taste
Cayenne to taste
1 tablespoon chopped parsley
1 egg, beaten
Bread crumbs

1. Make a thin white sauce with the butter, flour and cream.
2. Combine crabmeat, bread, mayonnaise, salt, cayenne and parsley. Stir in white sauce. If necessary soften with a little more cream. Shape into patties.
3. Dip into beaten egg diluted with a little water, roll in breadcrumbs and fry in deep fat until golden.

Crabmeat Casserole

1 green pepper, finely chopped
3/4 pound mushrooms, sliced
4 small sweet gherkins,
  chopped
2 tablespoons parsley,
  chopped
1-1/2 pounds fresh crabmeat,
  or 3 cans (7 ounces each)
  canned
6 tablespoons butter

5 tablespoons flour
1-1/2 cups milk, heated
1/2 cup light cream, heated
  with milk
1/2 teaspoon salt
Black pepper to taste
Cayenne pepper to taste
1/2 cup dry sherry
1/2 cup dry bread crumbs

1. Combine green pepper, mushrooms, gherkins, parsley and crabmeat.

2. In a saucepan melt butter, blend in flour, stir in warmed milk and cream. Cook, stirring until sauce is thick and smooth.

3. Add crab mixture to sauce. Season with salt, pepper and cayenne. Remove from heat and stir in sherry.

4. Spoon into buttered casserole, sprinkle with bread crumbs, dot with additional butter.

5. Bake in 350 degree oven for 30 minutes.

Crabmeat Imperial

1-1/2 pounds lump crabmeat
1/2 green pepper, finely diced
1 small jar pimento, chopped
1/2 teaspoon English mustard

1/2 teaspoon salt
1/4 teaspoon white pepper
1 egg, beaten well
1/2 cup mayonnaise

1. Carefully pick over crabmeat, remove shells. Mix remaining ingredients in a bowl. Add crabmeat carefully.
2. Pile lightly in one quart casserole. Coat with small amount of additional mayonnaise and sprinkle lightly with paprika.
3. Bake at 50 degrees for 25 minutes.

Ron's Crab Dip

16 ounces ketchup
2 to 4 tablespoons
  Worcestershire sauce
2 to 4 tablespoons lemon
  juice

1/4 teaspoon garlic salt
1/4 teaspoon onion salt
1/4 teaspoon celery salt
4 to 6 drops tabasco
a good handful crab

1. Mix all ingredients together in a large bowl and refrigerate.

   Prepare a day ahead of time for best flavor.

Potato Chip Dip

8 ounces cream cheese
1 heaping tablespoon mayonnaise
2 teaspoons onion and juice
   (grate)
1/4 teaspoon Worcestershire
   sauce

2 teaspoons parsley chopped
   (optional)
1-1/2 tablespoons lemon juice
1/4 teaspoon salt
4 drops tabasco sauce
3/4 cup cottage cheese
1 can clams or crab.

1. Mix all ingredients together in a small bowl and refrigerate.

   Prepare a day ahead of time for best flavor.
   This is a must for holiday gathering at my house.

Sand Dabs with Tomatoes and Shallots

1-1/2 pounds sand dabs, pan-dressed, Rex sole pan-dressed, OR 1-1/4 pounds Pacific sole fillets such as Petrale, Dover, or English or any firm, mild, white-fleshed Oregon trawl-caught fish
1 teaspoon olive oil
2 tablespoons finely chopped shallots

1-1/4 pounds fresh tomatoes, peeled, seeded and chopped
1 teaspoon grated ginger
2 tablespoons lime juice
2 teaspoons minced fresh cilantro
4 teaspoons chopped roasted cashews

1. Rinse fish with cold water; pat dry with paper towels.

2. In large skillet, saute shallots briefly in olive oil. Stir in tomatoes; cover and simmer for 5 minutes. Stir in ginger. Place sand dabs skin side down in skillet over tomato mixture. Cover and cook for approximately 6 to 8 minutes or until fish is opaque and no longer translucent. Transfer fish to serving platter leaving sauce in skillet.

3. Add lime juice to sauce and reduce to thicken. Top fish with sauce. Sprinkle with cilantro and cashews. Drizzle remaining lime juice over fish and serve immediately.

Serves four.

Breakfast

Larry's Breakfast Drink

6 ounces orange juice
8 ounces plain yogurt
1 banana

1 teaspoon honey
1/2 teaspoon vanilla

1. Mix all ingredients in blender until smooth.

German Pancakes

4 eggs
1 cup milk or light cream
1 cup flour
1/2 teaspoon salt

3 tablespoons powdered sugar
Dash nutmeg
Dash cinnamon
1 tablespoon butter

1. Preheat oven to 400 / 425 degrees.
2. Melt butter in a 9" x 13" pan in oven until bubbling.
3. In a blender, mix all ingredients except powdered sugar until foamy and smooth, right before pouring into pan.
4. Pour mixture into pan and bake 8 to 10 minutes.
5. Sprinkle powdered sugar on top just before serving.

Fancy Egg Scramble

1 cup bacon, ham or sausage,
  chopped
1 or 2 bunches green onion
3 tablespoons butter
12 eggs
1 can mushrooms

Cheese Sauce:
2 tablespoons butter
2 tablespoons flour
2 cups milk
1 cup cheese, grated
1/2 cup bread crumbs

1. In large skillet fry meat. Add onions and butter, saute lightly.
2. Add eggs and scramble lightly.
3. In medium skillet melt butter. Stir in flour. Remove from heat, and add milk slowly. Return to low heat and add cheese. Stir until blended and cheese is melted.
4. Pour eggs, cheese sauce and mushrooms into a flat baking dish. Top with bread crumbs. Cover and refrigerate until 30 minutes before breakfast.
5. Bake uncovered in 350 degree over for 30 minutes.

Bread

Barbecued Bread

1 pound bread dough; frozen
  from the store or your own
  recipe
Olive oil

Pinch salt
1 teaspoon dried herbs of your
  choice

1. Separate the dough into four equal pieces. Roll each piece into a 6-inch flat round, oil each side and place on a piece of foil (about 10-inches square). Let rise about 20 minutes, until puffy.

2. Bake over medium coals about 2 minutes on first side. Before baking second side, you can top the baked side with pizza toppings, cooked chicken or any pizza or sandwich-type filling.

Poppy Seed Coffee Cake

4 eggs, beaten
1/2 cup oil
1 cup water
1 package white or lemon
  cake mix
1 package instant vanilla or
  lemon pudding mix
1/4 cup poppy seeds

Topping:
1 teaspoon cocoa
1 teaspoon cinnamon
1/2 cup sugar

1. Beat eggs. Add oil, water, cake mix and instant pudding mix. Mix well. Fold in poppy seeds.
2. Topping: Mix together cocoa, cinnamon and sugar.
3. Grease and flour bundt or angel pan. Add 1/2 batter; cover with 1/2 topping. Add remaining batter and sprinkle with remaining topping.
4. Bake at 350 degrees for 50 minutes.
5. Let cake rest in pan for 15 minutes before removing.

Angel Biscuits

5 cups flour
1/4 cup sugar
3 teaspoons baking powder
1 teaspoon salt
1 teaspoon soda

1 cup shortening
1 package yeast
1/4 cup warm water
2 cups buttermilk

1. In a large bowl mix first five ingredients. Cut in shortening.
2. Dissolve yeast in warm water. Add buttermilk. Combine with first mixture.
3. Knead in bowl until combined. Roll out and cut into small biscuits. Let raise until double.
4. Bake at 400 degrees for 15 to 20 minutes.

Can be frozen on a cookie sheet and then packed in bags. Remove from freezer, thaw and bake as directed.

Porcupine Bread

1 package active dry yeast
3 to 3-1/2 cups bread flour
1/2 cup rolled oats
1 teaspoon salt
2 tablespoons sugar
1 cup buttermilk

1/2 cup water
2 tablespoons oil
1/2 cup raisins
1/4 cup sunflower seeds
2 tablespoons sesame seeds

1. In large mixer bowl, combine 1-1/2 cups flour, rolled oats, yeast, sugar and salt. Mix well.

2. Heat buttermilk, water, and oil until warm (120 to 130 degrees). Add to flour mixture. Blend at low speed until moistened; beat 3 minutes at medium speed.

3. By hand gradually stir in raisins, sunflower seeds, sesame seeds, and enough remaining flour to make a firm dough.

4. Knead on floured surface until smooth and elastic, 5 to 8 minutes (dough may be slightly sticky).

5. Place in a greased bowl, turning to grease top. Cover and let rise in warm place until double, about 1 hour.

6. Punch down dough. Form into loaf shape and place in a greased 9 inch by 5 inch bread pan. Cover and let rise in a warm place until double, about 1 hour.

7. Brush top of loaf with egg wash (1 egg blended with 1 tablespoon water). Sprinkle additional sunflower seeds and sesame seeds on loaf.

8. Bake at 375 degrees for 35 to 40 minutes until golden brown. Remove from pan and cool.

Flatbread

2 tablespoons warm water
1 teaspoon yeast
2 tablespoons yogurt
1/3 cup flour
2 teaspoons sugar

2-3/4 cups flour
2 teaspoons sea salt
1 tablespoons black onion
   seeds (kalaunji)
1 cup warm water

1. Stir together water, yeast and yogurt. Mix in 1/3 cup flour and sugar.
2. Leave overnight, or for at least 3 hours in an unlit oven. The mixture will bubble nicely until you are ready for it.
3. In a bowl combine 2 cups of flour, sea salt and black onion seeds. Add the yogurt starter and water.
4. Knead the dough on a floured board, kneading in additional 3/4 cup flour. Leave it to rise for 2 hours.
5. When the dough has doubled in bulk, divide it in half. Heat the griddle until it is hot. Flatten the dough as for pizza or roll it out and turn it onto the griddle. You want the bread to toast but not burn. When it is brown and speckled on both sides (this takes about 5 minutes), reduce the heat to low and continue to cook for about 10 minutes, until it sounds hollow when tapped.

Dilly Casserole Bread

1 cup all purpose flour
2 tablespoons sugar
1 tablespoon instant minced onion
2 teaspoons dill seed
1-1/4 teaspoons salt
1/4 teaspoon soda
1 package active dry yeast

1 cup creamed cottage cheese
1/4 cup water
1 tablespoon butter or margarine
1 egg
1-1/2 to 2 cups all purpose flour

1. Lightly spoon flour into measuring cup; level off. Combine first 7 ingredients in large mixer bowl.
2. Heat cottage cheese, water and butter in saucepan over low heat until warm (120 to 130 degrees).
3. Add egg and warm liquid to flour mixture. Blend at low speed until moistened. Beat for 3 minutes at medium speed.
4. Stir the rest of the flour into the batter to form a stiff dough.
5. Cover and let rise in a warm place until light and doubled in size, about 1 hour.
6. Stir down dough. Turn into a greased 1-1/2 or 2 quart casserole. Cover and let rise in a warm place until light and doubled in size, about 30 to 45 minutes.
7. Bake at 350 degrees for 35 to 40 minutes or until deep golden brown. Immediately remove from casserole. Brush with butter and sprinkle with coarse salt, if desired.

Old-fashioned Lemon Bread

1-1/2 cups all-purpose flour
1 cup sugar
1 teaspoon baking powder
1/2 teaspoon salt
2 eggs
1/2 cup milk
1/2 cup salad oil

1-1/2 teaspoons grated lemon peel

Lemon Glaze:
4-1/2 tablespoons lemon juice
1/3 cup sugar

1. In a large bowl stir together the flour, sugar, baking powder, and salt.

2. In a separate small bowl, beat the eggs with the milk, salad oil and lemon peel.

3. Add the liquid mixture to the flour mixture; mix just until blended. Pour batter into a greased and floured 5 inch by 9 inch loaf pan.

4. Bake at 350 degrees for 40 to 45 minutes or until pick inserted in center comes out clean.

5. Glaze: In a small pan heat lemon juice and sugar until sugar dissolves.

6. When bread finishes baking, use a long wooden skewer to poke numerous holes to bottom of loaf. Drizzle the hot glaze over top so it slowly soaks into bread. Let bread cool in pan about 15 minutes. Remove from pan and cool on a rack.

Mother Walpole's Whole Wheat Bread

2 packages dry yeast
1/2 cup warm water
4 cups hot water
1/4 pound margarine
2 tablespoons sugar

4 cups white flour
1 tablespoon salt
6 cups stone ground whole
   wheat flour

1. Blend yeast with 1/2 cup warm water. Let set for 10 minutes.
2. Blend hot water margarine and sugar. Add yeast.
3. Add white flour and salt. Beat until smooth and gluten is developed.
4. Add whole wheat flour, mix thoroughly. Turn out onto a floured board and knead until smooth.
5. Let rise 1-1/2 hours.
6. Punch down and let rest for 10 minutes.
7. Divide into four parts and make into loaves and let rise for 45 minutes.
8. Bake at 350 degrees for 35 minutes.

Makes four loaves.

Joan's Enriched Bread

4 to 4-1/2 cups of flour (all white or half whole wheat)
1 package quick-rise yeast
1/2 cup corn meal
1/2 cup oat bran

1/4 cup sugar
1 teaspoon salt
2 cups water
1/4 cup oil

1. Combine half the flour and the other dry ingredients – including the yeast – in a large bowl. Measure water and oil into the same container and pour over dry mixture. Mix until thoroughly incorporated. Add remaining flour to make a firm dough. Knead about 6 minutes, until gluten (elasticity) is well-developed.

2. Place in a greased bowl, turn to grease top. Cover; let rise in warm place until double, about 30 minutes.

3. Punch down. Form into two loaves, place in pans and allow to rise until double; 30 to 40 minutes.

4. Bake at 350 degrees for 20 to 25 minutes.

Cinnamon Rolls

3/4 cup milk
1/2 cup sugar
2 teaspoons salt
1/2 cup margarine
1/2 cup warm water
2 packages yeast
1 egg, beaten

4 cups flour

Icing:
1 cup sugar
1/2 cup whipping cream
1 teaspoon vanilla
1 tablespoon butter

1. Scald milk, stir in sugar, salt and margarine. Cool to lukewarm.
2. Measure warm water into large bowl. Sprinkle in yeast. Stir until dissolved.
3. Stir in milk mixture, egg and 1/2 flour. Beat until smooth. Stir in remaining flour to make a stiff batter. Cover with waxed paper. Refrigerate at least 2 hours. (Dough may be kept in refrigerator 3 days.)
4. Roll out dough 1/4 inch thick. Spread with butter, white sugar, and if desired brown sugar; sprinkle with cinnamon and raisins. (You may want to soften raisins first in hot water.) Roll and cut into 1-inch slices. Let raise on greased baking sheet until double in bulk.
5. Bake at 375 degrees for about 20 minutes.
6. Icing: combine sugar and cream and cook till it forms a soft ball when tested in cold water.
7. Add vanilla and butter, cool, and whip by hand until texture of honey.
8. Spread over rolls.
This sweet dough can be used to make hot cross buns.

Six-Weeks Treasure Muffins

4 eggs, well beaten
1 cup brown sugar
1 quart buttermilk
3/4 cup vegetable oil
1 package bran buds (15 ounces)

5 cups flour (use some whole wheat if you have it, about 1/20
5 teaspoons baking soda
2 teaspoons salt

1. Mix first 4 ingredients together. Add bran buds and set aside while you mix the remaining dry ingredients together. Add dry ingredients to mixture. Store in a covered container in the refrigerator. This batter will keep up to six weeks.

2. When ready to bake, fill greased or paper-lined muffin tins 1/4 full. Top with a treasure such as a teaspoon of jam or cream cheese and/or some nuts. Cover with more batter until muffin cups are 2/3 full.

3. Bake at 400 degrees for 13 to 16 minutes.

Rhubarb Crumb Coffee Cake

1/2 cup butter
1-1/2 cup brown sugar
1 egg
1 teaspoon soda
1 cup sour cream
2 cups flour
1-1/2 cups rhubarb, cut in 1/2
  inch pieces

1 teaspoon vanilla
1/2 cup nuts, chopped coarse

Crumb Topping:
1/2 cup brown sugar
1 teaspoon cinnamon
1 tablespoon butter.

1. Cream butter and brown sugar. Add egg and blend. Mix soda and sour cream and add to sugar mixture alternately with flour. Blend in rhubarb, vanilla and nuts last.

2. Pour into greased 9 inch by 13 inch pan.

3. Crumb Topping: Blend brown sugar, cinnamon and butter and crumble over cake mix.

4. Bake in at 350 degrees for 35 minutes.

Jam Bundt Cake

2/3 cup butter
1 cup sugar
10 ounces strawberry jam
3 eggs
1 teaspoon vanilla
2 cups flour
1 teaspoon salt
3/4 teaspoon soda
1 tablespoon cinnamon

1 teaspoon allspice
1/2 cup buttermilk
1 cup coconut

Brown Sugar Glaze:
2 tablespoons brown sugar
1 tablespoon butter
4 tablespoon milk
1 cup powdered sugar, sifted.

1. Cream butter and sugar. Add jam, eggs, vanilla and blend until smooth.
2. Mix dry ingredients, add, alternating with buttermilk. Fold in coconut.
3. Bake in a 325 degree oven for 55 to 60 minutes.
4. Cool for 10 minutes, remove from pan.
5. Glaze: Blend brown sugar, butter and milk in saucepan. Heat and stir until smooth. Add powdered sugar and beat until smooth.
6. Drizzle glaze over cake.

Refrigerator Rolls

2 tablespoons dry yeast
1/2 cup warm water
2/3 cup shortening
1/2 to 1 cup sugar
1 teaspoon salt

1 cup mashed potatoes
1 cup milk
2 eggs
6 cups flour

1. Dissolve yeast in warm water.
2. Mix all ingredients. Knead well. Let rise for 1 to 1-1/2 hours.
3. Punch down. Put in greased bowl, roll to cover with grease, refrigerate covered tightly. Can shape and let rise overnight in refrigerator.
4. Bake in 350 degree oven till golden.

Rich White Coffee Can Batter Bread

1 package active dry yeast
1/2 cup warm water
1/8 teaspoon ground ginger
3 tablespoons sugar
1 can evaporated milk (13 ounces)

1 teaspoon salt
2 tablespoons salad oil
4 to 4-1/2 cups flour
Butter or margarine

1. Dissolve yeast in water. Add ginger and 1 tablespoon sugar. Let stand in warm place until bubbly, about 15 minutes.

2. Add remaining sugar, milk, salt and oil. At low speed beat in flour 1 cup at a time. Beat in last cup of flour with spoon until dough is very heavy and stiff but too sticky to knead.

3. Place dough in two 1-pound or one 2-pound well greased coffee can. Cover with greased plastic lids. (May freeze at this point.)

4. Let rise until dough pops lids off. (One-pound cans 45 to 60 minutes; 4 to 5 hours if frozen. Two-pound cans 1 to 1-1/2 hours; 6 to 8 hours if frozen.)

5. Bake in a 350 degree oven for 45 minutes for 1-pound can, 60 minutes for 2-pound can. Brush tops with butter.

6. Let cool 5 to 10 minutes. Loosen crust with thin knife, let cool in an upright position.

Quick Butter Croissants

1 package dry yeast
1 cup warm water (about 110 degrees)
3/4 cup evaporated milk
1-1/2 teaspoons salt
1/3 cup sugar
1 egg
5-1/4 to 5-1/2 cups all-purpose flour, unsifted

1/4 cup butter or margarine, melted and cooled
1 cup firm butter or margarine, at refrigerator temperature
1 egg beaten
1 tablespoon water

1. In a large bowl dissolve yeast in water. Add milk, salt, sugar, egg and 1 cup of flour. Beat to make a smooth batter, then blend in melted butter. Set aside.

2. In a large bowl, using a pastry blender or 2 knives, cut the firm butter into 4 cups of flour until butter particles are the size of peas. Pour the yeast batter over top and carefully turn mixture over with a spatula to blend just until all flour is moistened.

3. Cover with clear plastic wrap and refrigerate for at least 4 hours or up to 4 days.

4. Turn dough out onto a floured board, press into a compact ball, and knead briefly to release air. Divide dough into 4 equal parts. Shape 1 part at a time, leaving remaining dough, wrapped in plastic wrap, in refrigerator.

5. On a floured board, roll dough into a circle, 17 inches in diameter. Using a sharp knife, cut circle into 8 equal wedges.

6. For each croissant, loosely roll wedges toward point.

Shape each roll into a crescent and place on an ungreased baking sheet with point down, 1-1/2 inches apart all around. Cover lightly and let rise at room temperature in a draft-free place. (Do not speed rising of rolls by placing them in a warm spot.)

7. Beat egg with 1 tablespoon water. When almost doubled (about 2 hours) brush with egg-water mixture. Bake at 325 degrees for about 35 minutes or until lightly browned.

Serve warm or let cool on racks.

Makes 32 croissants.

To reheat, arrange rolls (thawed, if frozen) in a single layer on baking sheet; place, uncovered in a 350 degree oven for about 10 minutes.

Incidentals

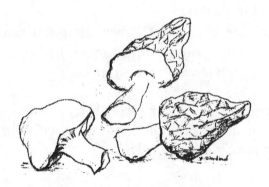

Merle's Mop Sauce

1 cup vinegar (cider or wine)
5 tablespoons Worcestershire
  sauce
2/3 cup vegetable oil
3 tablespoons butter
1 lemon, thinly sliced
2 to 3 cloves garlic, minced

3 tablespoons grated fresh ginger
2 tablespoons dry mustard
1 cup brown sugar (optional)
1-1/2 cups of ketchup (optional)

1. Put first eight ingredients into a saucepan and heat until the flavors are nicely blended. Use to baste any meat or poultry.

2. With the addition of brown sugar and ketchup, the mop sauce may be turned into a barbeque sauce to serve with meat after it is cooked.

Never baste anything you're barbecuing with a sauce that contains sugar or tomato. Both will burn and turn the meat black.

Olive-Pepper Caviar

2 jars (7 ounce) roasted red
  peppers
2 cans (6 ounce) pitted extra-
  large black olives.
1/4 cup olive oil

1-1/2 teaspoons minced garlic
1 teaspoon dried thyme leaves
1/2 teaspoon salt
Pepper to taste

1. Drain peppers and olives. Chop fine in food processor or with a sharp long-bladed knife. Transfer to a serving bowl.

2. Stir in olive oil, garlic, thyme, salt and pepper.

3. Serve with party breads or crackers.

Makes 3 cups.

Best Ever Beer Batter

1 cup white flour	1 tablespoon cooking oil
1/3 cup whole wheat flour	1 egg
1/4 teaspoon pepper	1 tablespoon baking powder
1 teaspoon salt	9 ounces (about) flat beer.

1. Mix first seven ingredients in a large mixing bowl.
2. Gradually add beer until it makes a thick batter.

The best batter ever for fish or vegetables. Try sliced zucchini and small, whole mushrooms as a better-than-fries accompaniment to fish — likewise battered.

Crème Fraîche

There is a delicious cream used in French cooking that is becoming increasingly popular (there's even an appliance on the market for making it) called crème fraîche or crème double. It's a wonderful rich topping for crepes, pies, and berries; just a spoonful will flavor gravies and sauces too. It has a slightly nutty, tangy taste, similar to that of sour cream, but a bit mellower.

1/2 pint sour cream   1 pint heavy cream

1. Heat creams over low heat until lukewarm.
2. Pour mixture into a small bowl; cover loosely with foil, waxed paper, or plastic wrap. Let stand until thickened, about six to eight hours at 75 degrees F, or longer at lower temperature; cover and refrigerate.
3. When supply is running low, just add more heavy cream (no need to add sour cream again) and repeat process.

Keeps about one week.

Dill-Mustard Sauce for Ham

2 tablespoons butter or margarine
2 tablespoons flour
1/2 teaspoon salt

1 cup milk
1/2 cup sour cream
1 tablespoon prepared mustard
1/4 teaspoon dill weed

1. Melt butter in saucepan.
2. Stir in flour and salt.
3. Add milk, slowly. Cook, stirring constantly until thick and smooth.
4. Stir in sour cream, mustard and dill weed. Continue heating very slowly until it reaches serving temperature.

Makes 1-1/2 cups.

Sweetened Condensed Milk

4 cups instant powdered milk
1 cup hot water
2 cups sugar

4 tablespoons margarine, melted

1. Mix all ingredients in blender.
2. Store in refrigerator.

Two reasons appear obvious for using this recipe — it's about 1/3 the cost of the canned version, and I sometimes need to make quickie fudge around midnight and loathe going to the store!

Steak Marinade

1 cup soy sauce
2 large onions, chopped
  coarsely
2 garlic cloves, halved

1/4 cup bottled gravy coloring
2 tablespoons beau monde
  seasoning

1. Combine soy sauce, onions and garlic in electric blender. Process on high for one minute or until very smooth.
2. Add gravy color and seasoning.
3. Refrigerate meat in marinade up to 24 hours. Marinade can also be used as a basting sauce.

Summer Ice Cubes

1 lemon   Water

1. Cut lemon into 16 pieces.
2. Place each piece of lemon, peel side up, into one section of ice tray. Pushing down on each one to extract the juice.
3. Cover with water and freeze.

This is a nice treat in colas or iced tea and to make "just plain water" not so plain.

Cucumber Salsa

4 pickling cucumbers, thinly
  sliced
Salt
1 small onion, halved length-
  wise, thinly sliced
1 hot red chili pepper, sliced

1 thin slice fresh ginger
1/3 cup seasoned rice vinegar
  or white wine vinegar
  mixed with 1/2 teaspoon
  sugar

1. Put cucumbers in a colander; sprinkle lightly with salt and let stand for 15 minutes. Rinse well and transfer to a small bowl.
2. Add remaining ingredients; cover and refrigerate at least 45 minutes before serving.

Preparation time: 10 minutes.
Standing time: 1 hour or more.
Yield: 3 to 4 servings.

Tortilla Chips

1 package tortillas, flour or
corn
2 tablespoons vegetable oil or
non-stick vegetable oil spray

Commercial or homemade
seasoning mix optional
(Mexican or other as pre-
ferred).

Conventional method:

1. Heat oven to 350 degrees.
2. Using a pastry brush or spray, lightly coat one side of each tortilla with oil, evenly stacking them oiled side up.
3. With a sharp or serrated knife cut stack into eighths. Separate the pieces and place them oiled side up on lightly greased baking sheets.
4. Bake for about 10 minutes or until just beginning to brown. Watch closely to avoid scorching.
5. If desired, toss with chosen seasoning blend.

Microwave method:

1. Omit oil and prepare two tortillas (16 chips) at a time.
2. Arrange on paper-towel lined plate.
3. Microwave, uncovered, on high power until crisp, about 3-1/2 minutes for flour tortillas or 3 minutes for corn tortillas.

These are low-fat and a good option for folks who want *big* chips for dipping.

Canning and Gift-giving

Bertha's Rhubarb-Strawberry Gelatin Jam

5 cups diced rhubarb
2-1/2 cups sugar
3 ounce package sugar free
   strawberry gelatin

1 package strawberry Kool-
   Aid
1/2 teaspoon margarine,
   optional

1. Mix sugar and rhubarb together. Let set for 30 minutes to an hour. (Juice will form to help prevent scorching while cooking.

2. Begin cooking on low heat, increase heat, stirring frequently, and bring to a boil. Simmer 10 minutes, stirring frequently. (I use a broad plastic spatula for stirring. It covers the bottom of the kettle better than a spoon.)

3. Remove from heat; skim and discard any foam or, if desired, add the margarine to suppress foaming.

4. Add gelatin and Kool-Aid; stir until dissolved.

5. Pour into clean freezer containers. Seal, label and freeze.

Cherry Variation: Substitute cherry gelatin and cherry soft drink powder for strawberry products.

Sauerkraut

Cabbage

2 teaspoon salt

1 teaspoon sugar

1 cup boiling water

Ingredients listed are for one wide mouthed canning jar of sauerkraut.

1. Fill jar half full of cut cabbage. Pack down.
2. Add 1 teaspoon salt and sugar.
3. Fill jar to neck with cabbage and tamp down again.
4. Make a hole in top of cabbage with finger. Add 1 teaspoon salt.
5. Seal with boiling lids.

Pickled Pig's Feet

1. Cook clean pig hocks in large kettle of water till tender. Add salt to water before boiling.
2. Have wide mouth gallon jar clean. Wash hocks off with cold water before putting in jar.
3. Fill jar with vinegar to cover. Let stand a few days for vinegar to pickle them.
4. Drain and serve with saltine crackers.

Rhubarb-Strawberry Puree

2 pounds rhubarb, cut into
 1-inch chunks to measure
 about 6 cups
1 cup sugar
1/2 cup pineapple juice

1 pound fresh strawberries,
 washed, hulled and coarsely
 mashed or sliced to measure
 about 2 cups

1. Combine all of the ingredients in a large non-aluminum pot.
2. Bring to a boil over medium-high heat, reduce to medium-low and simmer until thickened, about 25 to 35 minutes. stirring occasionally to prevent scorching.
3. Let mixture cool, then puree in food processor until very smooth.
4. Refrigerate up to 1 week, or spoon into freezer containers and freeze, allowing about 1 inch head space.

Yields about 4 cups.

Pickled Ginger

3 cups (about 1/2 pound) peeled ginger root, cut into slivers about 2 inches long

2-1/2 cups rice vinegar
2 teaspoons honey
2 teaspoons red miso

1. Soak ginger in ice water, covered, overnight.
2. In a stainless steel or enamel pot, combine vinegar, honey and miso. Bring to a boil.
3. Drain ginger, pack in 4 half-pint jars and cover with boiling liquid. Leave about 1/2 inch head space in each jar.
4. Seal and process in a boiling-water bath for 10 minutes.
5. Serve with roasted meats, in salads and with hot or cold noodles.

Seafood Seasoning Mix

3/4 cup salt
1 tablespoon white pepper
1 tablespoon black pepper
1 tablespoon garlic powder

1 tablespoon thyme flakes
1 tablespoon oregano, crushed
1 tablespoon sweet basil

1. Mix all ingredients.

Bottle in containers with shaker tops.
Makes a great gift.

Desserts

Coconut Cream Pie

3 cups milk
2/3 cup sugar
1/2 teaspoon salt
3 tablespoons cornstarch
2 tablespoons flour
3 egg yolks
1 tablespoon butter
2 teaspoons vanilla

1 cup Angel Flake coconut

Topping
1/2 pint whipping cream
2 tablespoon (heaping) powdered sugar
1 teaspoon vanilla

1. Heat milk to "hot".
2. Beat sugar, salt, cornstarch and flour into milk. Cook until thick.
3. Blend egg yolks. Add 3/4 cup of heated mixture into egg yolks and beat until well blended.
4. Add egg mixture into mixture on burner and blend together well.
5. Remove from heat, add butter, vanilla and coconut. Blend well.

Topping:
1. Beat whipping cream until it starts to thicken.
2. Add sugar and vanilla and beat until stiff.

Mother Howard's Inimitable Chocolate Pie

1 graham cracker crust, 9 inch
18 marshmallows
1/2 cup milk

6 Hershey bars, 1 ounce size
1/2 pint whipping cream

1. Cook first four ingredients in double boiler over medium heat until chocolate and marshmallows melt. Cool.
2. Whip cream.
3. Fold cooled mixture into whipped cream.
4. Pour into pie shell. Chill 2 to 3 hours.

Pineapple Cheesecake

Crust:
1 cup sifted all-purpose flour
  (sift before measuring)
1/4 cup sugar
1 teaspoon grated lemon peel
1/2 teaspoon vanilla extract
1 egg yolk
1/4 cup butter or margarine,
  softened

Filling:
5 packages (8 ounce size)
  cream cheese, softened
1-3/4 cups sugar
3 tablespoons flour
2 teaspoons grated lemon peel

1-1/2 teaspoons grated orange
  peel
1/4 teaspoon vanilla extract
5 eggs
2 egg yolks
1/4 cup heavy cream

Pineapple Glaze:
2 tablespoons sugar
4 teaspoons cornstarch
2 cans (8-1/4 ounce size)
  crushed pineapple in heavy
  syrup, undrained
1 tablespoon lemon juice
2 drops yellow food color

1. Preheat oven to 400 degrees. Grease inside of 9-inch springform pan (3 inches high). Remove side.

2. Make crust: In medium bowl, combine flour, sugar, lemon peel, vanilla. Make well in center; with fork, blend in yolk and butter. Mix with fingertips until smooth.

3. On bottom of pan, form half of dough into ball. Place waxed paper on top; roll pastry to edge of pan. Remove paper. Bake 6 to 8 minutes, or until golden. Cool.

4. Meanwhile, divide rest of dough into three parts. Cut six strips of waxed paper, 3 inches wide. On dampened surface, between paper strips, roll each part 2-1/4 inches wide and 9 inches long. Assemble springform

pan with crust on bottom. Line inside of pan with pastry strips, overlapping ends. Remove waxed-paper strips. Preheat oven to 450 degrees.

5. Filling: In large mixer bowl, blend cheese, sugar flour, peels and vanilla at high speed. Beat in eggs and yolks, one at a time, beat until smooth, occasionally scraping bowl with spatula. Beat in cream. Pour into pan. Bake 10 minutes. Lower oven to 250 degrees.

6. Bake 1 hour more. Remove to rack to cool — 2 hours.

7. Glaze: In small saucepan, combine sugar and cornstarch. Stir in remaining ingredients. Over medium heat, bring to boiling, stirring; boil 1 minute, or until thickened and translucent. Cool.

8. Spread surface of cheesecake with glaze; refrigerate until well chilled — 3 hours or overnight.

9. To serve: Loosen pastry from side of pan with spatula. Remove side of springform pan. Garnish with sliced strawberries, if desired. Cut into wedges.

Serves 16.

Toll House Pie

2 eggs
1/2 cup all purpose flour
1/2 cup sugar
1/2 cup firmly packed brown
sugar
1 cup butter, melted and
cooled to room temperature

1 cup milk chocolate chips
1 cup chipped walnuts
1 unbaked pie shell (9-inch)
Whipped cream or ice cream
optional.

1. Preheat oven to 325 degrees.
2. In large bowl, beat eggs until foamy; add flour, sugar and brown sugar; beat until well blended. Blend in melted butter. Stir in chocolate chips and walnuts. Pour into pie shell.
3. Bake at 325 degrees for 1 hour.
4. Remove from oven. Serve warm with whipped cream or ice cream.

Makes one 9-inch pie.

Recipe may be doubled. Bake two pies, freeze one for later use.

Orange Chiffon Pie

1/2 cup sugar
1/2 teaspoon salt
1 envelope plain gelatin
1 cup cold water

3 eggs separated
1/2 cup undiluted frozen
   orange juice, thawed
1/4 cup sugar

1. Mix first four ingredients in sauce pan. Cook over direct heat stirring constantly until dissolved. Remove from heat.

2. Slightly beat egg yolks to which a little of the hot mixture has been added and blend into remaining hot mixture. Cook over boiling water until mixture coats a metal spoon. Usually about three minutes.

3. Remove from heat. Add orange juice. Chill until thickened but not set.

4. Beat egg whites until foamy. Add sugar. Continue beating until meringue stand in stiff glossy peaks when beater is raised. Gently fold into cooked mixture.

5. Pour into baked crust and chill.

6. Garnish with whipped cream and walnuts.

Strawberry Pie

1 pie shell, baked
8 ounces cream cheese (low
  fat if you desire)
2 to 3 boxes strawberries,
  washed and hulled

Glaze:
1 cup sugar
3 tablespoons cornstarch
2 tablespoons lemon juice

1. Line cooled pie shell bottom with softened cream cheese.
2. Cover cream cheese with whole berries (1 to 2 boxes).
3. Glaze: Crush 1 box of berries in sauce pan. Add sugar and cornstarch. Cook to clear, thick stage. Remove from heat. Add lemon juice.
4. Pour glaze over berries in pie. Cool.
5. Top with whipped cream.

Deluxe Chocolate Marshmallow Bars

3/4 cup butter or margarine
1-1/2 cups sugar
3 eggs
1 teaspoon vanilla extract
1-1/3 cups all purpose flour
1/2 teaspoon baking powder
1/2 teaspoon salt
3 tablespoons baking cocoa
1/2 cup chopped nuts, optional

4 cups miniature marshmallows

Topping:
1-1/3 cups (8 ounces) chocolate chips
1 cup peanut butter
2 cups crisp rice cereal

1. In a mixing bowl, cream butter and sugar. Add eggs and vanilla; beat until fluffy.

2. Combine flour, baking powder, salt and cocoa; add to creamed mixture. Stir in nuts if desired.

3. Spread in a greased jelly roll pan. Bake at 350 for 15 to 18 minutes.

4. Sprinkle marshmallows evenly over cake; return to oven for 2 to 3 minutes. Using a knife dipped in water, spread the melted marshmallows evenly over cake. Cool.

5. Topping: Combine chocolate chips, butter and peanut butter in a small sauce pan. Cook over low heat, stirring constantly, until melted and well blended. Remove from heat; stir in cereal. Spread over bars. Chill.

Makes about 3 dozen bars.

Chocolate Syrup Brownies
with Chocolate Buttercream Frosting

Brownies:
2 eggs
1-1/2 cups packed brown
  sugar
1-1/2 cups chocolate syrup
3 cups flour
1/2 teaspoon baking soda
1/4 teaspoon salt
1 cup butter, melted

1 cup, heaping, chopped walnuts or pecans

Frosting:
6 tablespoons boiling water
1/4 cup butter
3 teaspoons vanilla
1/2 cup cocoa
3 cups powdered sugar

1. Brownies: Beat eggs, sugar and syrup together. Sift flour, baking soda and salt together and add to sugar mixture. Fold in butter and nutmeats last.

2. Spread in well-greased 9 by 13 inch pan. Bake at 350 degrees 38 to 45 minutes – until just underdone.

3. Frosting: Add boiling water to butter. Mix in vanilla and cocoa. Beat with a wooden spoon until well blended. Add sugar and beat until smooth and creamy. Add a little milk if mixture is too thick.

4. Spread frosting on warm brownies.

Fudge-Butterscotch Suicide Cake

1 German chocolate cake mix
 – no pudding
1 can sweetened, condensed
 milk
1/2 jar Mrs. Richardson's
 fudge-butterscotch topping.

1 package of Cool Whip topping (8 ounce size)
2 Heath candy bars (4 individual bars), crushed

1. Bake cake as directed in a 9 x 13 inch pan.
2. While cake is hot, poke a meat fork into the cake about 20 time and pour milk over the cake.
3. Pour, over the top, budge-butterscotch topping. Let the cake cool.
4. Frost with Cool Whip and sprinkle with crushed Heath bars just before serving.

Christian Church Apple Crisp

Filling:	Topping:
6 - 8 sliced golden delicious apples	1 cup sugar
1 cup sugar	1 cup flour
1 teaspoon nutmeg	1 cup margarine
1 teaspoon cinnamon	1 cup oatmeal
4 tablespoons flour	1/2 teaspoon nutmeg
	1/2 teaspoon cinnamon

1. Mix together all filling ingredients and pour into greased 9 x 13-inch dish
2. Blend all topping ingredients with pastry cutter to resemble crumb topping. Spread over apple mixture.
3. Bake at 350 degrees for 45 minutes. Cool.

Served topped with Cool Whip or ice cream.

Blackberry Cobbler

1/2 cup butter
1 quart blackberries
1 cup flour
1 cup sugar

1/2 teaspoon salt
2 teaspoons baking powder
1 cup milk

1. Preheat oven to 350 degrees. Place butter into a 7 x 11-inch baking pan and set it into the oven and let the butter melt.
2. Mix the dry ingredients. Add milk and blend vigorously.
3. Pour into pan with melted butter. Sprinkle blackberries over batter.
4. Bake for 45 minutes to 1 hour.

Serve with ice cream or whipped cream.

Iola's Oatmeal Cookies

1 cup butter
1 cup white sugar
1 cup brown sugar
2 eggs
2 cups flour
1 teaspoon baking soda

1 teaspoon baking powder
1 teaspoon salt
1 teaspoon vanilla
2 cups quick oats
1 cup coconut, shredded

1. Cream together butter and sugars.

2. Add eggs and beat well.

3. Sift together flour, baking soda, and baking powder then add to mixture a little bit at a time, mixing well.

4. Add in the last four ingredients, mix gently but thoroughly.

5. Lightly grease cookie sheet and drop dough by spoonful.

6. Bake at 350 degrees for 8 to 10 minutes.

Gilded Lily Apple Crisp

1/2 cup unsifted all-purpose flour

1/2 cup firmly packed light brown sugar

8 tablespoons butter (1 stick)

1/2 cup coarsely chopped walnuts (2 ounces)

1/4 cup raisins

1/4 cup semisweet chocolate pieces — or 1/4 cup coarsely chopped semisweet chocolate

5 large pie apples, such as Cortland or Golden Delicious (about 2-1/2 pounds)

2 tablespoons brandy, bourbon or cream sherry

1. Preheat oven to moderate (350 degrees).

2. Combine flour and brown sugar in large bowl. Cut in 6 tablespoons of the butter with pastry blender until mixture resembles coarse meal. Gently stir in nuts, raisins and chocolate until thoroughly mixed.

3. Pare, core and coarsely chop apples. Place in a 2-quart casserole.

4. Melt remaining 2 tablespoons butter in small saucepan. Stir in brandy. Scrape over apples; toss until coated. Top with raisin-nut mixture.

5. Bake in 350 degree oven until apples are soft and the topping is lightly browned, about 40 minutes. If topping browns too quickly, cover loosely with aluminum foil tent. Serve immediately.

Barb's Molasses Cookies

3/4 cup margarine
1 cup sugar
1/4 cup molasses
1 egg
2 cups flour

2 teaspoons baking soda
2 teaspoons cinnamon
1/2 teaspoon cloves
1/2 teaspoon salt

1. In large mixing bowl beat together first four ingredients.
2. Add dry ingredients and mix well.
3. Drop on ungreased cookies sheet.
4. Bake at 350 degrees for 8 minutes.

Pumpkin Squares

1 can pumpkin (16 ounces)
1 can condensed milk (13 ounces)
3 eggs beaten
1 teaspoons pumpkin pie spice

1/2 teaspoon salt
1 cup sugar
1 package yellow cake mix
1/2 cup margarine (1 cube)

1. Combine first 6 ingredients and pour into 9" x 13" pan.
2. Cut margarine into cake mix and sprinkle over batter.
3. Bake at 350 degrees for 30 to 40 minutes. When cooled, store in refrigerator.

To order additional copies of

Peanut Butter Sticks
To The Roof Of Your Mouth

Please send _____ copies at $12.95 for each book, plus $3.50 shipping and handling for the first book, $2 for each additional book.

Enclosed is my check or money order of $_____
or [ ] Visa   [ ] MasterCard
#_____ Exp. Date _____/_____
Signature _____
Phone _____

Name _____
Street Address _____
City _____
State _____ Zip _____

(Advise if recipient and mailing address are different from above.)

For credit card orders call:
1-800-895-7323

or

Return this order form to:

BookPartners
P.O. Box 922
Wilsonville, OR 97070